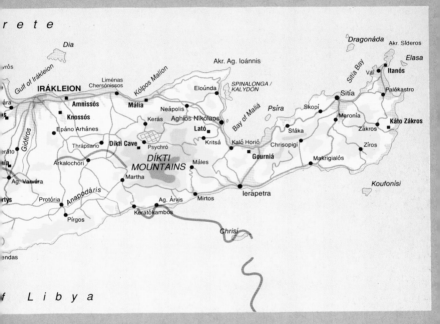

r e t e

Dia

Dragonáda

Akr. Sideros

vrós

Gulf of Irákleion

Elasa

Sitía Bay

Vaï

Itanós

Liménas
Chersónissos

Kólpos Malíon

Akr. Ag. Ioánnis

Palékastro

IRÁKLEION

Eloúnda

SPINALONGA /
KALYDÓN

Sitía

Amnissós

Mália

Neápolis

Aghíos Nikólaos

Psíra

Skopí

Maronía

Káto Zákros

Knossós

Kerás

Bay of Mallá

Stáka

Zákros

Epáno Arhánes

Lató

Gídhiros

Kaló Horió

Chrisopigi

Zíros

ráto

Thrápsano

Díkti Cave

Psychró

Kritsá

Makrigialós

aja

Arkalochóri

DÍKTI
MOUNTAINS

Gourniá

Ag. Varvára

Máles

Koufonísi

Anapodáris

Martha

Ierápetra

rtys

Protória

Ag. Árvis

Mirtos

Keratókambos

Pírgos

Chrisi

endas

f L i b y a

INSIGHT *Pocket* GUIDES

CRETE

Written and Presented by **Brigitte von Seckendorff-Kourgierákis**

INSIGHT
Pocket
GUIDES

Insight Pocket Guide:

CRETE

Directed by
Hans Höfer

Managing Editor
Andrew Eames

Photography by
María Sirí

Design Concept by
V. Barl

Design by
Willi Friedrich

© 1994 APA Publications (HK) Ltd

All Rights Reserved

Printed in Singapore by
Höfer Press (Pte) Ltd
Fax: 65-8616438

Distributed in the UK & Ireland by
GeoCenter International UK Ltd
The Viables Center, Harrow Way
Basingstoke, Hampshire RG22 4BJ
ISBN: 9-62421-523-5

Worldwide distribution enquiries:
Höfer Communications Pte Ltd
38 Joo Koon Road
Singapore 2262
ISBN: 9-62421-523-5

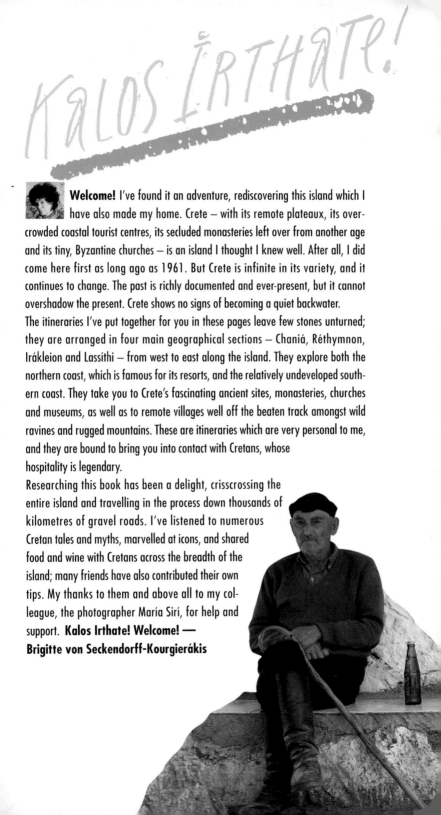

KALOS IRTHATE!

Welcome! I've found it an adventure, rediscovering this island which I have also made my home. Crete – with its remote plateaux, its over-crowded coastal tourist centres, its secluded monasteries left over from another age and its tiny, Byzantine churches – is an island I thought I knew well. After all, I did come here first as long ago as 1961. But Crete is infinite in its variety, and it continues to change. The past is richly documented and ever-present, but it cannot overshadow the present. Crete shows no signs of becoming a quiet backwater.

The itineraries I've put together for you in these pages leave few stones unturned; they are arranged in four main geographical sections – Chaniá, Réthymnon, Irákleion and Lassíthi – from west to east along the island. They explore both the northern coast, which is famous for its resorts, and the relatively undeveloped south-ern coast. They take you to Crete's fascinating ancient sites, monasteries, churches and museums, as well as to remote villages well off the beaten track amongst wild ravines and rugged mountains. These are itineraries which are very personal to me, and they are bound to bring you into contact with Cretans, whose hospitality is legendary.

Researching this book has been a delight, crisscrossing the entire island and travelling in the process down thousands of kilometres of gravel roads. I've listened to numerous Cretan tales and myths, marvelled at icons, and shared food and wine with Cretans across the breadth of the island; many friends have also contributed their own tips. My thanks to them and above all to my col-league, the photographer María Sirí, for help and support. **Kalos Irthate! Welcome! —
Brigitte von Seckendorff-Kourgierákis**

Contents

*Preceding pages:
the fortress of Irákleion*

What to Know

Following pages:
the waterfront at Chaniá

From Minóa to King Minos

Crete (*Ee Kreétee* in Greek) was, in antiquity, densely forested with cypress, cedar, oak, juniper and plane trees, as well as various varieties of pines and palms. In his poetry, Homer refers to 'Knossós of the many trees' as well as to the heavily wooded Mount Ida range. Crete was a green paradise which did not actually become an island until around a million years ago, when segments of the mountain range connecting the Peloponnese (southern Greece) with what today is Turkey sank below sea level. Where did the first human settlers of the region come from? The scientific community has not yet reached a concensus on this point, but they probably originated in Asia Minor, Africa or, perhaps, predynastic Egypt. Whatever the origins of the first Cretans, the island was populated during the Neolithic Age as early as the 7th century BC.

The Palace of Knossós

Culture

Schliemann's discovery of Troy – which established the historical validity of Homer's epic poetry – followed by the discovery of Knossós by the Cretan scholar Kalokerinós, triggered off a veritable frenzy of excavation. Digging at Knossós from 1900–03, the English archaeologist Arthur Evans made a crucial discovery. Instead of the expected Mycenaean remains, Evans unearthed a great building complex, a palace, which he recognised to be the centre of an even older civilisation. He proceeded to name this 'new' culture 'Minoan', after that powerful and wily monarch of Greek mythology, King Minos, though no image of him ever turned up at Knossós, nor any other evidence that a 'King Minos' had played a central role in the culture which was to bear his name.

'The King of Priests'

What Evans did find were renderings, in various media, of decidedly female figures. After initially trivialising them, he eventually concluded 'that we are looking at a great monotheistic cult in which the female form of deity occupied the highest position...' The Minoan goddess, a sister of the numerous moon- and mother-goddesses of Asia Minor, later metamorphosed into the Greek goddess Rhea. Her symbol was the double axe, or 'labrys'; trees were consecrated to her; and she was also worshipped in the form of a snake in the island's private homes. There are numerous references in ancient legend to the priestess-queen, Minóa, the 'Female Ruler of the Labyrinth'.

In around 3000BC, paralleling the civilisations of Egypt and Mesopotamia, a great culture evolved on Crete which is thought to have been the first such flowering in Europe. The older 'palaces', erected in around the year 2000, were destroyed some 300 years later. Subsequently, new, similar complexes were built atop the ruins on the same sites. The 'palaces' were major economic, political and religious centres, and Homer placed their number at 100. Multi-storeyed, they included workshops, large storerooms, places of worship, areas reserved for social functions, courtyards, theatres,

Fresco from Knossós

plumbing and sewage facilities, as well as projecting and receding façades. Later Greek conquerers of Crete were so bewildered by this architecture that they coined the word 'labyrinth' – from 'House of Labrys'. The Minoan system of writing – in hieroglyphs and syllabary form, scratched onto clay tablets, or written in ink on papyrus and leather – has been only partially deciphered, but, a culture capable of developing writing and such sophisticated art and architectural forms as that of the Minoans may be considered to have attained a high level of civilisation and prosperity.

As early as the 12th century BC, the Dorians, a rough breed of uneducated semi-barbarians, were on the advance throughout Greece, bringing war to the once peaceful island and enslaving its inhabitants. The Minoans, men and women alike, retreated into the mountains, founding new cities there. From this point on, Crete belonged firmly in the Greek world. The Greek goddesses and gods supplanted the island deities – above all, the divine Olympian patriarch, Zeus, whose birthplace Crete was thought to be. In this embodiment however, Zeus became immortal along the same lines as the partner of the Great Goddess: he died or was sacrificed in the autumn and then rose again in the spring. As this heretical belief in Zeus's 'resurrection' was incomprehensible to them, the mainland Greeks defamed the Cretans, coining the maxim 'All Cretans are liars'.

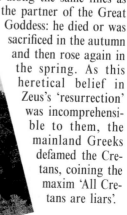

Foreign Intervention

During the 1st century, the Roman commander Metallus acquired the epithet 'Creticus' by breaking the Cretans' stalwart three-year resistance, incorporating them into the Roman Empire. The island then became the granary of the empire and an important military base, as well as ripe ground for the spread of Christianity. During the 7th and 8th centuries, Rome was subjected to increasingly effective attacks by the Slavs, Persians and Arabs. Then, in the year 1204, in a very understated transaction, Crete was sold to the Republic of Venice for 10,000 silver marks. The indigenous population put up a bitter resistance for 200 years but did not succeed in throwing off foreign rule.

After the conquest of Constantinople by the Turks in 1453, many intellectuals and artists fled to Crete, which led to a final, late florescence of Byzantine art and culture on the island, influenced by the Italian Renaissance. The painters Domenikos Theotokópoulos, ('El Greco'), and Michaïl Damaskinós belong to this period, as does the poet Vitzéntzios Kornáros, author of the epic drama, *Erotókritós*, in addition to the playwright Yiórgios Chortátzis.

Candia, as the Venetians called the modern capital of Irákleion, the most formidable fortress in the Mediterranean, was compelled to surrender to the Turks in 1669. Islamisation made rapid progress. The so-called *Turkokrítes* were Cretans, as far as their clothing, language and customs were concerned, but they professed the Moslem faith. The island was divided up among pashas and large landowners, trade and agriculture fell off, and the Renaissance ended.

Despite these demoralising developments the Turkish forces were faced with constant resistance. This period of struggle, of mass executions and rebellion, is kept alive in many stories still told on the island; and in songs singing the praises of those 'brave young men', the *palikária,* and their feminine counterparts, the *levéntisses.*

The Turkish Fortress of Aptera

The year 1821 marked the beginning of the struggle on the Greek mainland for liberation from the Ottoman yoke – up in 'old Greece', as elderly Cretans still often call it. While Greece became a free state, at least on paper, the Turks continued to savagely suppress all rebellion on Crete. In 1866, 1,000 people, barricaded in the Arkádi Monastery, ignited an ammunition dump and blew themselves up rather than fall into the hands of the Turks besieging them. When an additional massacre of Christians in Irákleion took place, the English consul was among those killed and the European powers responded with outrage, sending in ships and declaring Crete autonomous. As a result, the Turkish military was forced to leave, but the island remained under Turkish sovereignty.

In 1899, the first Cretan government was sworn in: Elefthérios Venizélos, Chaniá's favourite son and later prime minister of Greece, was named Minister of Justice. For a brief period, Chaniá became a small European capital – acquiring the cosmopolitan flair which it has retained until today.

Meanwhile, the island was 'protected' by international armed forces: the Nomós, or Prefecture, of Chaniá by the Italians; Nomós Réthymnon by the Russians; Nomós Irákleion by the English, and Nomós Lassíthi by the French. This authoritarian system paved the way for another revolution in 1905, but Crete did not become part of the Greek state until 1913, since which time it has remained a stronghold of progressively-orientated parties, from the Liberals and the Centre Party to today's PASOK, the Greek socialists.

In 1913, King Constantine and Prime Minister Venizélos came to Chaniá to ceremoniously proclaim Crete's official union with Greece. The remaining Turkish population, some 33,000 strong, had to leave the island immediately.

The Air Invasion

Four days after the Greeks' surrender to the German military, 20 May 1941, marked the beginning of one of the most bitter chapters in Cretan history. This was when Hitler launched operation 'Merkur', which involved dropping thousands of German soldiers by parachute onto Crete in order to capture it as a supply base for the Afrika Corps. Before the soldiers were able to free themselves from their parachutes, however, they had become easy marks for

German military cemetery at Máleme

British and Cretan soldiers, the latter armed primarily with knives and clubs. The retaliation of the German Wehrmacht was swift: villages were razed, cities bombed and male inhabitants executed. Memorial plaques all over Crete testify to these tragic events. On 11 October 1944, Irákleion was handed over to the Cretan partisans. Western Crete, however, remained occupied until 8 May 1945.

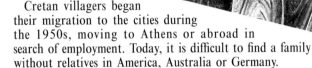

Cretan villagers began their migration to the cities during the 1950s, moving to Athens or abroad in search of employment. Today, it is difficult to find a family without relatives in America, Australia or Germany.

In 1951, the United States built military bases near Chaniá and Irákleion. A new occupation had begun – controversial and much criticised to this day. Another 'invasion', in the form of the Colonels' military dictatorship also affected Crete. During the junta, from 1967 to 1974, many islanders were persecuted, imprisoned and tortured along with liberals and democrats throughout the rest of Greece.

Resistance, in one guise or another, has long been the central theme in Crete's history, since the decline of the peaceful Minoan society till today. The much-sung, often banned Cretan 'anthem' expresses the islanders' longing for freedom and peace in such lines as: 'When will the sky be free of clouds? When will February come; spring...?' But considering Crete's pivotal geographical position between Africa, Asia and Europe, poised above the turbulent Middle East, a future free of foreign intervention seems unlikely.

The Extended Cretan Family

In spite of increasing urbanisation and the staggering boom in tourism, the four regions of Crete, blocked off by three imposing massifs, have maintained their own customs and dialects. The period of migration is over, and some of the emigrants have even begun to return. Since 1971, the population has steadily increased to its present level of 520,000. Today, tourism, agriculture, trade and industry provide enough jobs to keep the Cretans at home.

The island has also become an attractive destination for Athenians keen on escaping the polluted capital with its smog, traffic and overcrowding. Intellectual life on Crete is characterised by the multitude of cultural associations, as well as by the university, founded in 1977. Since the school maintains separate campuses in Chaniá, Réthymnon and Irákleion, wags sometimes call it 'the longest university in the world'.

With its tight network of social relationships, Cretan society retains the feeling of one big extended family. The Greek tradition of *koumbariá,* a sort of elective kinship system involving 'best men' and godfathers, creates interrelationships as binding as those based on blood. For the Cretan politician intent on securing a following and consolidating power, it is essential to stand in as godfather to as many island children as possible. It is this that makes him a *sínteknos,* a co-parent. By sharing the responsibility for a child, he acquires a new family (of voters). In this scheme of things, weddings and baptisms are highly significant social events. Often attended by hundreds of guests, there is always plenty of eating, drinking and dancing at these celebrations. The *paniyíria*, or saints' day festivities, are also important occasions. On the eve of the celebrations, people throng to the church or monastery sacred to the saint to light their candles in anticipation of the feast day to follow. The Greek Orthodox Church has always played an important rôle on Crete and continues to do so. In the past, during the centuries of foreign rule, it was the Church which preserved the Greek language and culture, and the priests played a leading role in the Cretan resistance.

On Crete, time, as we know it in the West, does not exist. 'Right away', 'soon', and 'in five minutes' are assurances that can rarely be taken at face value. They may just as well mean 'in half an hour'. Information concerning distances should also be treated with a healthy dollop of suspicion, along with street directions. The Cretan clock marches to a very different drummer. Long mornings are followed by siesta time which lasts from around 2 until at least 5pm, when the Cretans rise and the 'afternoon' begins. Shops reopen, employees return to their offices, lawyers and physicians resume their practices, and people pay visits. At about 8pm it is time for the evening stroll, or *vólta*. A sort of 'see and be seen parade',

Sitía's city centre

the *vólta* has long served as the village marriage market, with prospective brides and suitors displaying their wealth and advertising their availability in shady squares and over cups of Greek coffee at seaside cafés. The rest of the evening, from 9pm on, is spent at the cinema, the theatre, at a concert or dining with one's special circle of friends, one's *paréa*, or relatives. Cretans may even schedule dinner for much later. It is a relaxed social event that is never rushed, and *'Na seh kerásso,'* ('Let me serve, or treat, you.') is the first sentence you should learn in Greek. It is the key to polite social behaviour in the land of hospitality. When Cretans sit down to dine, no one would think of refilling only his own wineglass. First, you serve your companions; then yourself. Hospitality is extended just as naturally as it is expected in return.

The Tourist Trade

Crete has the largest amount of tourist trade of all the Mediterranean islands, with a 14 per cent growth rate. From April to October well over a million holidaymakers visit the island. Germans predominate, followed by Scandinavians and the English.

The travel craze has two sides. On one hand, it produces a certain affluence and is therefore welcomed by the islanders. On the other hand, the locals view the overwhelming influx of summer visitors as a kind of hostile occupation force. Often, the much-praised Cretan hospitality is at risk of degenerating into a simple business arrangement, with the visitors contributing their share to this sad development. It is difficult for tourists to intuit the rules of hospitality in an alien culture, and well-meaning guests may fail to reciprocate kindnesses tendered by Cretans. What becomes more and more difficult as a result of this eroded relationship between guests and hosts is achieving any real access to the people and their island.

Tourist ghettos have evolved, entire towns avoided by the local population and abandoned in winter. This precludes the very dialogue and exchange which the enlightened traveller seeks wherever he goes; the meeting of minds that is the first, essential step in understanding the history and culture of Crete. An afternoon in a so-called 'real' Cretan village, built specifically for tourists, or an organised 'Cretan Evening' are no substitutes for the sort of encounter that is today difficult to experience if one stays in a resort.

Bathing fun at Chersónissos

As throughout all of Greece, music and song play an integral role in Cretan life. The oldest Cretan songs are the *risítika*. Written in the foothills of the Léfka Ori, the White Mountains, as early as the 10th century, they have since spread throughout the island. They are meant to be sung at the *távla*, the richly decked table, but also on the *stráta*, the street, on the occasion of the 'collecting' of the bride, for example. The songs recount heroic deeds, dreams of freedom, the beauty of the bride, and other stock themes of Cretan life. Popular songs at parties are *matináthes*, whose lyrics consist of rhyming couplets, often composed on the spot, with everyone joining in for the chorus. Of Italian origin are the principal musical instruments in use on Crete today: the *lyra,* a three-stringed, plucked instrument, and the accompanying lute. Larger ensembles, however, also use the violin, mandolin, guitar, bagpipes, wind instruments and small drums, whereas the straight flute, perhaps the oldest of Cretan instruments, has all but disappeared.

The place to go if you want to listen to indigenous music, dance and have a good meal while you are at it is a *kritikó kéntro*, one of those large restaurant-clubs catering for weddings and other celebrations, located outside the towns. The Cretan dances are elegant and fast: the *sirtós, pentosáli* and *malevisiotikos* are all round dances; only the *soústa,* which dates from the Venetian occupation, is danced by couples.

Crete is, in fact, one large mountain range, and its people were once semi-nomadic, mounting mules and riding up to the highland villages in summer. The many weekend outings with one's *paréa* usually end on Sunday evening in the *kafeneíon* of some mountain village; at the home of a *koumbáros* or *sínteknos* who has prepared *kokinistó*, a kid goat steamed in a wine and tomatoe sauce; boiled *stamnangáthia*, a type of wild dandelion and the most expensive wild vegetable on Crete; and *paximáthia*, double-baked barley rusks soaked in water, then covered in oil, tomatoes and *rígani*, wild oregano. The repast may include the hard cheese, *graviéra*, and the finest Greek soft cheese, *athótiros*. To drink with the meal, you have your choice of wine from the barrel, or the local brand of anise-flavoured schnapps, *tsigouthiá*, the Cretan 'national' drink.

In the streets of Cretan towns and villages, one still occasionally sees an elderly man in boots and baggy breeches, a crocheted, fringed scarf tied artlessly around his head – the antique garb of Moslem and Christian Cretans both. The men's beautiful old regional costumes, with their finely embroidered waistcoats, and the elaborate gowns of the women are today worn only at staged events and consigned to display cases in folklore museums. Young Cretans, like their Western counterparts, now prefer jeans, athletic shoes, T-shirts and jackets embossed with international labels. However, at the same time, the Orthodox priest, the *papás*, in his long black soutane and conical hat is by no means exotic, especially now that he is allowed to wear his hair and beard short. He may be married – only the higher-level clergy remain celibate – have children, and knows quite well what life in the real world is like.

There are plenty of reasons for wanting to visit Crete, but once you have, a return trip is inevitable. In the words of Nobel prize winner, Odysséus Elytis, who was born in Irákleion in 1911: '…take me, take me to Crete, and do not ask, do not ask me why.'

Iearápetra, south coast city

HISTORY

BC

6500–3000 Neolithic Age, first settlers arrived from Asia Minor or North Africa.

3000–2050 Prepalatial Period, processing of copper and use of the potter's wheel.

2050–1625 Early Palatial Period, discovery of bronze, written language developed. Destruction of the old palaces.

1625–1375 The Late Palatial Period, and Late Minoan era, flourishing Minoan culture dominates the seas. Palaces are destroyed in 1375.

1375–1000 Post-Palatial Period, Crete participates in the Trojan war. Beginning of the Iron Age, marked by the arrival of the Dorians and the retreat of the Eteocretans into the mountains.

1000–67 Dark Ages, founding of Dorian towns and constant internecine feuding. In 145, Pressós, last Eteocretan town and largest pirates' lair in the Eastern Mediterranean, falls.

AD

67BC–AD337 Crete becomes a Roman province under Metallus 'Creticus'. Górtis becomes capital city and Christianity spreads. Titus named first bishop of Crete.

337–826 Crete's first Byzantine period, following the division of Rome. Crete falls to Byzantium and pirate raids became rife.

827–961 Arabs occupy Crete, destroying Górtis and founding Rabdh el Khandak (Irákleion), where a slave market flourishes.

961–1204 Second Byzantine period, Crete reconquered by Byzantine General Phokás, era of military administration, rechristianisation and establishment of the feudal system. Sea trade is in the hands of the Genoese; the capital is called Chándax (Irákleion).

1204–1669 Venice purchases Crete, expelling the Genoese, and renaming Chándax Candia. Venetian colonists flood in, but their rule is marked by uprisings, corsair raids and expanded fortifications. All but Candia eventually conquered by the Ottomans.

1669–1898 Candia falls to the Turks in 1770 after a 20-year siege. An uprising led by Daskaloyánnis is suppressed.

1821–1828 Crete participates in the Greek struggle for independence. In 1850, Chaniá becomes capital; in 1866, the tragedy at Arkádi occurs, leading to further popular uprisings.

1898–1913 Some autonomy is gained when, still under the Sultan, the island is protected by the major powers. Moslem Cretans leave. Crete redoubles its efforts to join Greece.

1913–41 Crete unites with Greece following Balkan Wars, entering World War I on the side of the Entente. Turks leave in 1923.

1941–5 The German Occupation, heavy losses, destruction of many villages and mass executions.

1944–9 Greek Civil War is fought less fiercely than on the mainland.

1967–74 Military dictatorship.

1972 Irákleion becomes capital.

1981 Greece joins EC; elects a socialist government helped by Crete's massive left-wing support.

1990 Conservative Néa Dimokratía government, headed up by Cretan-born prime minister Mitsotákis, resolves to move US military bases from the mainland to Crete, resulting in large-scale demonstrations and clashes with Athenian police.

Crete is divided up into four administrative regions, or *nómi*. Visitors arrive at one of the district capitals – Chaniá, Réthymnon, Irákleion or Aghios Nikólaos, which then serves as their point of departure for the excursions. But please do not take any of our well-made plans too literally: an itinerary which can easily be accomplished in half a day, you yourself may wish to extend. An occasional detour off the beaten path will almost always be worth your while, even if it takes you down a bad gravel road or two.

Chania

Not Just Quinces and Cheese: The Arab geographer and historian Al-Sarik Al-Edrisi, who travelled throughout the island during the 12th century, reported the following: 'The island of Crete, large, densely populated and fertile, has many flourishing cities.' One of

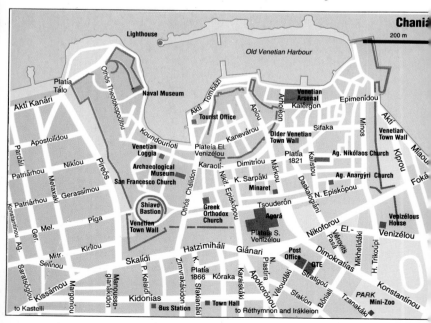

Chaniá

200 m

Lighthouse

Old Venetian Harbour

Platía Tálo
Akti Kanári
Óthos Theolokopoúlou
Naval Museum
Akti Tombázi
Apíou
Arholéon
Venetian Arsenal
Kalérgon
Epimenídou
Akti Kíprou
Tourist Office
Kanevárou
Sifaka
Minos
Venetian Town Wall
Miaou
Koundourióti
Older Venetian Town Wall
Apostolídou
Venetian Loggia
Platía El. Venizélou
Kalistou
Ag. Nikólaos Church
Foká
Pardáli
Nikíou
Pireós
Archaeological Museum
Karaolí-
Dimitríou
Márkou
Platía 1821
Ag. Anargýri Church
Patriárhou
Metaxáki
Gerassímou
San Francesco Church
Óthos Chalídon
Nikit. Episkópou
K. Sarpáki
Minaret
N. Episkópou
Daskalogiáni
Patriárhou
Píga
Shiavo Bastion
Greek Orthodox Church
Tsouderón
Venizélous House
Konstantínou Ag.
Mel.
Venetian Town Wall
Agorá
Nikofórou
El.-
Venizélou
Ger-
Mitr. Selínou
Kirílou
Hatzimiháli
Giánari
Platía S. Venizélou
Váyovits Pasá
Mikhelidáki
H. Trikoúpi
Skalídi
P. Kelaidí
Zimvrakákidon
Post Office
Dimokratías
Saratsóglou
Kissámou
Margoníou
Mangusso-gianákidon
Kidonias
Platía 1866
Kóraka
Stakalanáki
Karaiskáki
Apokorónou
Váyoudáki
Plastíra
QTE
Stratigoú
Bónali
Konstantínou
PARK Mini-Zoo
Tzanakáki
to Kastelli
Bus Station
Town Hall
Stakíon
to Réthymnon and Irákleion

The harbour at the foot of Kastélli

these urban centres, surrounded by fruit orchards and hills full of wild goats, he called Rabdh-el Djobh, the 'City of Cheese'.

Chaniá's cheese still merits a mention. But 'Kydonía', the oldest name for the town, derives from the word for quince, a fruit probably introduced from Asia as early as Minoan times. In Ancient Greek myths, the entire region was said to be inhabited by the ancestors of the Kydones, ruled by King Kydon, a son of Minos renowned for his hospitality. Chaniá is thus one of the oldest settled areas in Europe, a fact confirmed by the discovery of an extensive settlement complex on the city's hill, Kydonía, in 1970. As a Roman province, Chaniá was a flourishing community, minting its own money and maintaining a theatre. Later, the Byzantines made the city the seat of a diocese. The name Chaniá itself may derive from *al hanim*, the Arabic word for inn. The Venetians then italianised it, coining the name 'La Canea'.

In 1645, it was the first Cretan city to fall to the Turks, serving as an Ottoman foothold in the conquest of the rest of the island. During the next few centuries, Chaniá assumed the economic leadership of the entire island and, in 1850, it became the seat of the Seraskeri Pasha, the highest pasha. Chaniá experienced its true heyday, however, as the seat of government and capital of autonomous Crete between 1898 to 1913. The quarter of Chalépa, with its fine neoclassical architecture, dates from this period.

Chaniá, Crete's capital until 1972, is growing quickly and, with its population of 63,000, is second only to Irákleion in size. Chaniá is a city full of vitality and plenty of green, with clean air and substantial recreational facilities. From here, you have easy access to the surrounding villages, to the Lefká Ori, the White Mountains, to secluded coves along the south coast, as well as the broad sandy beaches of the West.

A First Encounter

Old harbour and Venetian quarter; Fort Firkás; the monastery church of San Francesco and the Archaeological Museum; the joys of shopping in the covered bazaar.

It is a good idea to find accommodation in the vicinity of the old harbour, where there are countless hotels, pensions, restaurants and bars. (See 'Accommodation' in the *What to Know* section.) The old Venetian quarter is classified as a protected, historic precinct and the Greek authorities have made a successful job of renovating it. At the height of summer, the quarter becomes the focal point of tourist activity in Chaniá.

You begin to get a feel for the district by setting out from **Plateía E Venizélou**, also called Sintriváni, and proceeding west along the harbour promenade, **Topanás**, to the Venetian-Turkish battlements of **Fort Firkás**. This is not only the location of the **Maritime Museum**: in summer, theatre groups stage guest performances and Cretan dance evenings here. From the ramparts of the fort, you have a panoramic view of the harbour, the Venetian arsenals and the former Mosque of the Janissaries, all the way to the White Mountains, 2,500m (8,202ft) high.

Next to the lighthouse you will find the ruins of a fort which was the former execution site of the Venetians and Turks. There is a striking mountain slope some distance from here to the east, which Kazantzákis' hero, Alexis Zorbas – in his incarnation as Anthony Quinn – brought to the attention of the world. On a hill facing you lies **Kastélli**, the oldest district of Chaniá, with the palatial **Venetian Archives**, today part of the Technical University. From the vantage point of Fort Firkás, you will also discover the palate of Cretan colours: from delicate yellow and ochre to pink. West is **Aghios Theóthoros**, an island nature reserve protecting the rare Cretan wild goat, or *kri-krí*. The shoreline road round the fort leads

Independence Day parade, 28 October

to the northern bastion of the Venetian town wall with the state-owned **Xenia Hotel**. The adjoining thoroughfare, **Othós Theotoko-poúlou**, and the other small streets here are lined with numerous Turkish houses. Here, you will also find Venetian houses and plenty of little shops and restaurants. And not far away is the **Schiavo Bastion**, located in a well-preserved section of town wall, with a moat on the other side.

On **Othós Chálidon**, the street with the most souvenir shops, you will find the **Archaeological Museum** – in the former Venetian monastery church of **San Francesco** – which houses finds which span Crete's long eventful history. The church and museum are equally worth your time and attention. Diagonally opposite, in the former Turkish bathhouse, a coppersmith has his workshop. At the end of Othós Chálidon is **Plateía 1866**, also called Néa Katastímata, a square lined with trees, where you can find a taxi or a bus to the old seaside resort of Kalamáki. One of the oldest *kafeneía,* or traditional cafés, in town is located across the square on the corner.

Ee Agorá, the covered bazaar on **Plateía S Venizélou**, is a compact shopper's paradise. Vegetables, fruit, fish, meat, spices, cheese, wine, mountain teas, snack bars and a *kafeneíon* – you can find anything and everything here. There are 78 shops and stands in all and, in the middle, a *períptero*, or kiosk, selling newspapers, books, maps and small items such as chewing gum and cigarettes. The cross-shaped market building, begun in 1911 and unique in Greece, was patterned after the covered market in Marseille, one of Chaniá's major trading partners during the Turkish period.

Opposite the mar-

ket **Othós Tsanakáki** begins, its upper part lined with trees. This is one of the city's main streets, and the post office, telephone exchange (OTE), travel agencies, Olympic Airways and many small boutiques, are located here. The **Dimotikós Kípos**, featuring a gorgeous, old-style *kafeneíon*, is an inviting place to relax a while, its open-air cinema a destination for movie lovers in summer.

The **Historical Museum**, with its comprehensive collection and second-largest archives in Greece, is located above Othós Sfakianáki 20 in a lovely neoclassical building. On **Plateía Eleftherías**, at the end of the street, there is another beautiful example of neoclassical architecture, the seat of the High Court of Justice as well as of the *Nomarhía,* the prefecture of Chaniá. From here, you can follow **Othós Dimokratías** back to the market, passing the stadium and the municipal park. North-east of the market, **Plateía 1821** is the former centre of the Turkish Quarter, surrounded by Turkish coffee houses, the sky pierced by the minaret which once belonged to the Sultan Ibrahim Mosque. In 1912 the mosque was converted into an Orthodox church.

Further to the east, you have the nearly 5m (16ft) high Byzantine-Venetian town wall, surrounded by houses. **Othós Kanneváro** will take you by the Greek-Swedish

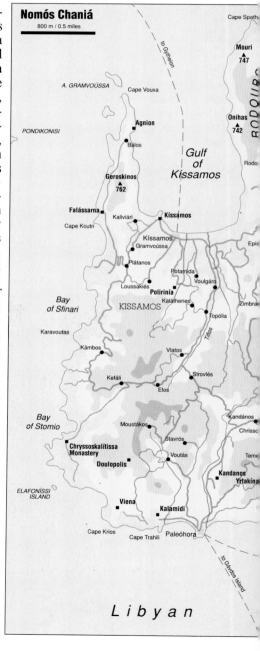

Nomós Chaniá

800 m / 0.5 miles

Cape Spath
to Gýthelon
Mouri ▲ 747
A. GRAMVOÚSSA   Cape Vouxa
Agnion
PONDIKONISI
Bálos
Onihas ▲ 742
Rodo
Gulf of Kíssamos
Geroskinos ▲ 762
Falássarna   Kíssamos
Kaliviári
Cape Koutri
Kíssamos
Gramvoússa
Epis
Plátanos
Potamida
Voulgáro
Loussakiés
Polirinía   Kaláthenes
Bay of Sfinari   KISSAMOS
Topólia
TIROS
Zimbra
Karavoutas
Kámbos
Vlatos
Kefáli
Strovlés
Elos
Bay of Stomio
Moustákos
Kandános
Chrisso
Stavrós
Chryssoskalítissa Monastery
Voutás
Teme
Doulopolis
Kandanos
Yrtakina
ELAFONÍSSI ISLAND
Viena   Kalamidi
Cape Krios   Cape Trahili   Paleóhora
to Gávdos Island
Libyan

excavations in **Plateía Ekateríni**. This dig, excavated between 1969 and 1984, eventually provided sensational proof that western Crete was once the centre of Minoan civilisation. From here, it is not far to the eastern harbour with its seven – once 23 – arsenals, its wharves and winter quarters for the galleys. At this point, you may decide it is high time for a break at one of the many *tavérnes* – the humble and traditional Greek restaurants – or cafés.

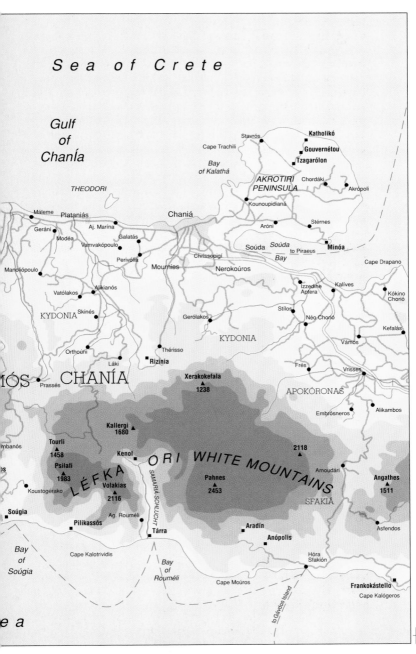

In the Mountains of Sfakiá

The Omalós Plateau; Samariá National Park, Europe's longest ravine; the wild coast of Sfakiá; the Askífou Plateau with its wonderful cheese. A day-long trip.

Located at an elevation of 1,080m (3,543ft), between the districts of Kydonía, Sélino and Sfakiá, the **Omalós Plateau**, with its 25km^2 (9.7 square miles), provides grazing land for numerous flocks of sheep. In addition to grain and potatoes, a variety of herbs thrive here. Inhabited only in summer, there are small hotels, private rooms and several *tavérnes*, in winter the snow is a metre deep.

There are several buses leaving daily from the KTEL bus terminal in Chaniá. The route runs via Alikianós, through orange and olive groves and the mountain village of Lákki on to the plateau. The Omalós is surrounded by the peaks of the **Léfka Ori** range, the tallest of which, Páchnes, rises to a height of 2,452m (8,044ft). With its three points of access easily defendable, this plateau was long considered the heart of Cretan resistance. Only twice did Turkish troops manage to advance this far. Set out on your day's journey as early as possible – preferably the evening before and not during the peak tourist season. Off season and in the early light, these marvellous mountains are seen to their best advantage. The **Tsani Cavern**, approximately 2,500m (2,734yds) long, is to the northeast. In autumn, the *katomerítes*, or lowlanders, come up here to pick the tender *stamnangáthi*, a sort of thorny dandelion plant.

The Omalós Plateau is the starting point for a hike through the longest and most famous (18kms/11 miles) ravine in Europe: the **Samariá Gorge**, in the national park by the same name. The Ancient Greeks believed that this precipitous gorge was the source of the light brought mortals by the god Apollo. It is open to the public (April–October, 6am–6pm), though sometimes closed due to flooding. The descent begins at the **Xylóskala** at the end of the asphalt road.

In peak season, up to 2,000 people trek

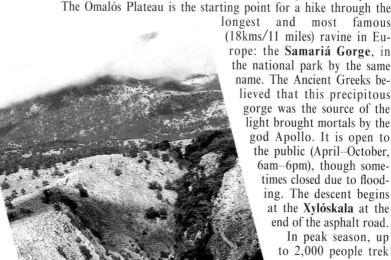

through the ravine every day. Nevertheless, you should not miss this wild mountain landscape, still the natural habitat of the indigenous wild goat, the *krí-krí*; and of eagles, falcons, buzzards and lamb vultures. About halfway through the ravine you will come upon the deserted settlement of **Samariá**, once the Venetian Santa Maria and, further down, the church of Osiá María Aegyptía, with its frescoes dating from the 14th century. In 1770, following an uprising in Sfakiá, thousands of women and children sought refuge here. The walls of the ravine, rising up to 60m (195ft) high, are only 3m (3.3yds) apart at the narrowest point.

The trail crosses the creek several times and there is a lot of scree on the way, so you should wear sturdy walking shoes for this hike! At kilometre 13 (mile 8), the end of the national park, a welcome sight awaits you: a kiosk selling drinks. Passing the ruins of the old village, you reach the new **Aghiá Rouméli** with its *tavérnes* and pensions. In ancient times this is where Cretan cypress wood was exported to Egypt. Today, small boats provide regular service to **Hóra Sfakión**, the 'capital' of the region of Sfakiá. From there, the last rural bus to Chaniá departs at 7pm.

It is a wild coastline, with mountains dropping off sharply into the deep blue sea, receding here and there to reveal a tiny cove. The history of Sfakiá is just as wild as the topography, and the people are considered to be the proudest, most freedom-loving and hospitable on the island – but also the sort one would not like to be at odds with. During the Ottoman Occupation, Sfakiá still retained the wealth it had gained from sea trade and piracy. The numerous uprisings, however, left it largely impoverished, and it is still the most sparsely populated region on Crete. In 1877, the Turks destroyed **Hóra Sfakión**. Considered to be at 'the end of the world' some 25 years ago, the town has a large number of *tavérnes,* hotels, pensions and rooms to rent clustered around the small harbour.

Heading back north, the road passes through the wild **Imvros Ravine** and the heartland of Sfakiá, the **Askífou Plateau**, at an elevation of 1,730m (5,675ft), surrounded by the tallest peaks of the **Léfka Ori**. Seven settlements overlook the plateau, much like spectators seated in an amphitheatre. The plateau, which provides the only land access to Sfakiá, is a fruit and wine-growing region and the cheese is wonderful. We recommend you give the *sfakianés pítes* with honey a try!

Kíssamos: Monasteries, Churches and Beaches

The Goniá Monastery above the sea; a special church in Episkopí; the Chrysoskalítissa Monastery with the legendary 'golden step'; dining under the mulberry trees. A day-long trip.

The road west to **Kastélli/Kíssamos** passes through plenty of green countryside, especially the stands of bamboo, from which the natives weave baskets, fashion fishing poles and sun roofs, and carve flutes. In the centre of Máleme, there is a fork in the road. The southern fork will take you to the spaciously laid out German military cemetery, the final resting place of 4,465 men.

The route continues via Tavronítis to **Kolimbári** with its fish restaurants. Overlooking the sea at the edge of town, you will find the Venetian **Goniá Monastery**, which was built between 1618–34 but has been destroyed numerous times. Inside the church, located in the middle of a courtyard, you will find one of the most important icon collections on Crete. A cannonball in the wall of the apse is just one reminder of the monastery's long and turbulent history.

Michaïl Arkángelos Church in Episkopí

The Michaïl Arkángelos Church near the town of **Episkopí** is worth a detour. Beautifully restored, it is the only rotunda on Crete, dating back to the 7th, 8th or 10th century. The next stretch on the winding road to Kastélli takes you through a silvery olive grove. From here a ship leaves once a week for Kythira and the Peloponnese. The road forks off to the south to **Polirínia**, a small village built into the side of the mountain. Wherever you turn, you see pieces of stone from the ancient town which once lay high up on the mountain. There is not much left of it, but the view alone – out over the **Gulf of Kíssamos**, flanked by the peninsulas of Rothopoú and Gramvoússa – is worth the half hour's climb up the mountain. (In midsummer, do not attempt this between noon and 6pm!)

The route from Kastélli to **Plátanos** is paved; after that, a gravel road weaves its way down to **Falássarna**, the former port of Polirínia, with its glorious beach. Here, too, greenhouses for tomatoes and cucumbers have begun to sprawl across the landscape. Little remains standing of the ancient town and not much else has been uncovered yet. There is no overlooking the 'throne' along the way. There are two small *tavérnes* where you can take a breather.

Continuing south from Plátanos, the road winds high above the sea, leading (unpaved from Kámbos on) through a number of pretty villages bedded in green. In Kefáli, you can turn off for Elafoníssi (but not before, if you want to avoid an adventurous, and time-consuming, trek across fields along the coast).

Positioned atop a rocky outcropping the **Chryssoskalítissa Monastery** is visible from a great distance. The westernmost point on Crete, in ancient times this was a place of refuge for the shipwrecked. A legend tells of 90 steps here, one of them made of gold, and invisible to sinners. Hence, the derivation of the name: Monastery of the Virgin of the Golden Step. A single nun and a monk inhabit the monastery today, the official explanation for this being that a man is required to hold mass. Actually, this chaste cohabitation is not only common practice, but also sanctioned by episcopal authority.

Chryssoskalítissa Monastery

Elafoníssi, the small island with the white dunes, is probably the only island in the world which you reach without the help of bridge or boat. The sea surrounding it is so shallow. Against the barren, karstic landscape it hovers like a delicate dream. On the other hand, it is here that the *lívas*, the Saharan wind, churns up the tallest waves in the Mediterranean. In 1907, they took their toll on the *Imperatrice,* which belonged to the Austrian Lloyd shipping line. The victims were buried on the island. On Easter Sunday, 1824, they say, the sea turned red here when 850 women and 40 men were slaughtered by the Egyptian troops of Pasha Ibrahim.

As the summer progresses, the 'mainland' beach gets more and more littered, partly due to illegal camping and partly to outright abuse of the environment. The road back to Chaniá via Kefáli and **Elos** – the Cretan chestnut capital, with its annual Chestnut Festival (third Sunday in October) – takes you through the wild ravine near **Topólia**. Just before reaching Kolimbári you can stop at **Bárbas Leftéris** in **Kimissianá** for some splendid dining under the mulberry trees – they serve sumptuous Cretan specialities and wine from the barrel.

To Sélino in the Southwest

A charming drive, crossing the mountains to the south, with time off for a swim. A half- to full-day excursion.

You may extend this outing to a full day, especially if you decide to stop for a swim. This route appears quite long on the map, but it consists almost entirely of well-paved, wide roads, first west towards Tavronítis, and south from there towards Paleóhora. The thrill of driving from the north to the south on Crete is crossing the mountains to the Libyan Sea. The landscape, cultivated since Minoan days, is characterised by endless olive groves.

Kandanós, on a slope stretching all the way to Paleóhora, is a village with no charm and a sad history. A commemorative stone in the village square is a tragic reminder of the destruction of the village in 1941 by the German Wehrmacht.

Paleóhora is a pleasant little town on the southern coast, still unspoilt by mass tourism. Boats ply between here and Hóra Sfakíon, as well as to the tiny island of **Gávdos**, Calypso's isle and the southernmost point in Europe. There is a sandy beach stretching out to the west of the town, and a pebble beach to the east. You will find plenty of hotels, pensions and private rooms here. There are fish restaurants on the harbour and at the foot of the ascent to the Fortezza at the southernmost point of the beach, as well as the sophisticated **Fortezza Restaurant**, with its marvellous view of the sea and mountains. The most beautiful hotel is the old **Libykó** at the entrance to town. Many of the guests come from the island of Gávdos. On the road to Soúgia, you can stop for a rest at **Asogirés**, a tiny town in a green valley with several *kafeneía*. Not far away, you can visit the tiny museum in a monastery erected in honour of the '98 holy fathers', the *Aghiï Patéres*. Nearby, you may also seek out the 'miracle tree', one of the few

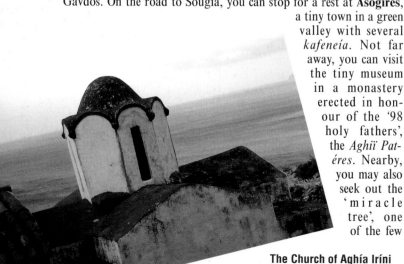

The Church of Aghía Iríni

View of Paleóhora

evergreen plane trees on Crete. According to legend, the holy fathers in their cave up on the mountain all breathed their last at precisely the same time as Holy Ioánnis O Xénos (John the Foreigner), because they had left him behind on the little island of Gávdos on their way to Crete from Egypt. Here, too, the locals celebrate on 7 October the 'forgotten' saint's name day with a big festival, or *paniyíri*. On the road to Soúgia, below Teménia, you will find an architectural gem: the **Church of Sotíros Christoú**, with its groin-vaulted dome. Originally a small fishing village on a wide pebble bay, Soúgia today is a popular resort and excursion destination. High up on the hill, the Church of **Aghía Iríni** (12th century) with its groin-vaulted dome, has a stunning view of the surrounding landscape.

On the drive back to Chaniá, you can make a stop at the turn-off for the village of Sémbronas for some hot food and locally made wine by the carafe at the **Kafeneíon Sémbronas**.

The Akrotíri Peninsula

An array of monasteries; a visit to Bear Cave; the lively little port of Soúda. A half-day tour.

There is more to see than monasteries on the peninsula north-east of Chaniá, though they alone are well worth a trip to this lovely (and strategic) area. Chaniá is expanding rapidly onto the peninsula, but while more and more holiday villages are popping up on the west coast, the east and south, in contrast, are characterized by military zones – NATO and US bases sealed off from the public. Near Stérnes, is Chaniá airport as well as the military airfield.

From Chaniá, drive uphill towards the airport and, once you have attained the heights, stop – at the **Venizélos Graves** located in the middle of the park grounds. Elefthérios Venizélos was Chaniá's

British military cemetery near Soúda

favourite son, scion of one of Greece's most important political families. After his death in Parisian exile in 1936, he was buried here with his son, Sophoklís. With the Léfka Ori towering above it, this park offers one of the lovliest views of the city below.

Just before the turn-off for Soúda in Korakiés, look for a small road on your left which leads to the **Kalogreón (Moní) Monastery**, a convent with a well-kept courtyard full of flowers, and a place of tranquillity and beauty. The nuns here sell beautiful, handwoven table-cloths.

The road then heads past the airport to the **Aghía Triátha Monastery**, the convent's big brother, which dates back to the beginning of the 17th century. The Renaissance façade is a visual symphony of pink and red – particularly picturesque in the light of the setting sun. Consecrated to the Holy Trinity, the church is situated in the middle of an arcaded courtyard, and the monastic complex contains a collection of valuable icons and other art treasures.

Your route continues via a gravel road up the mountain to the **Gouvernéto Monastery**, the exterior of which greatly resembles a fort. This monastery dates from the 16th century, and the church, with its splendid façade, is consecrated to the All-pure Virgin (*Ee*

Aghía Triátha Monastery, Akrotíri

Panagheía). On 6 and 7 October here, the local residents pour into the courtyard to celebrate a religious festival, or *paniyíri*.

A half-hour's walk down the mountain will bring you to the long-abandoned **Katholikó Cave Monastery**, past the **Bear Cave**, which served as a place of worship as early as the late Stone Age. After first climbing along the opposite side of the Akrotíri Peninsula, the road finally returns to Soúda by way of the airport. At the end of Soúda Bay, you will come upon a reminder of things past, the British military cemetery holds 1,527 graves of British soldiers who died defending Crete during World War II.

Soúda is a lively little port, its daily rhythm determined by the departures and arrivals of ferries to and from Piraeus. Fifteen kilometres (9 miles) long, Soúda Bay is one of the finest natural harbours in the Mediterranean. For this reason, it has long been valued as a site for naval bases.

A tree-lined road now takes you back to Chaniá but, just before you reach town, there is a boulevard on the left leading to the very beautiful, renovated convent of Chrissopigí (The Golden Spring), dating from the 16th–17th century. The fact that candles alone illuminate the church here makes for a very special atmosphere, especially during evening services (*esperinós*).

Stérnes on the Akrotíri Peninsula

Yoghourt and Honey

The remains of Aptera; 'tsigouthiá' in Samonás and yoghourt and honey in Vrísses; the charming villages of Vámos. Half-day tour.

High above the entrance to Soúda Bay, on an artificially created plateau, the ancient city of **Aptera** was located. The headland's strategic location was unique – but it was also representative of the type of site chosen by the bellicose Dorians: it was impossible for ships to approach Aptera unnoticed. The city, which grew wealthy as a result of maritime trade, reached a pinnacle of influence in the 3rd century BC. It was discovered in 1834 by the English traveller, Pashley, and later excavated by Italian archaeologists. The harbour lay on the opposite side of the bay, in what today is Maráthi and was called Minoá in antiquity.

The road to Aptera branches off from the National Highway. The city's name, which means 'wingless', is said to date back to a contest between the Sirens and the Muses. Overcome by grief at their loss, the Sirens tore off their wings and fell into the sea, metamorphosing into the islands which separate Soúda Bay from the open sea. On the drive up the mountain, keep your eyes open for Roman cisterns along the way, as well as for a Turkish **fortress** erected in 1816.

On the road to Stylos, just before you reach the town, look for the **Church of Panagheía Serviótissa**, which dates from the 11th–12th century, situated in the middle of an orange grove. It has an octagonal dome which is unique on Crete. **Stylos**, a small village surrounded by greenery, is well-known for its mineral water. From here, the road branches off to Samonás, from which a gravel road leads to one of the island's most beautiful Byzantine churches, **Aghios Nikólaos** (near Kyriakosélia) dating from the 11th–12th

Almirída and Pláka

From Aptera, a view of the former prison

century. In **Samonás**, a stop at the small, *kafeneíon* is a must. Order a Greek coffee or a *tsigouthiá,* Crete's anise-flavoured version of *oúzo* (Be careful: it's strong!), and ask for the key to the church.

Your next stop is **Vrísses**, a town situated beside a stream under mighty plane trees, where you can enjoy fresh yoghurt with honey. Heading out of town in the direction of Chaniá, the road forks off to the right towards Vámos, and winds up the mountain. Halfway up, you will see the small, deserted **Karídi Monastery**, which belongs to the wealthy Aghía Triátha Monastery on the Akrotíri Peninsula. The monks' cells have collapsed, and **Aghios Geórgios,** flanked by two mighty walnut trees in the middle of the courtyard, is today a simple country church.

Gavalohóri

There are many charming villages around **Vámos**: **Gavalohóri**, which belonged to the Byzantine Gavaládon family, is very pretty with all its restored houses; as are Aspro, Pláka and Kókkino Horió. A natural place for a rest on the way back to Chaniá is **Kalíves**. The little restaurant (*estiatório*) called **Sorbás** is a good bet.

Réthymnon

'Réthymnon is a small town… They used to say, in the old days, that its trade was praiseworthy, its shipping flourished and, what is more, that a few good poets and painters were born here.' Thus Pandelís Prevelákis, well-known even outside Greece for his skill as a novelist, begins his chronicle of life in Réthymnon, his home town. In return, in 1987, a year after the writer's death, the town honoured him with a monument erected in front of the town hall.

Painted entirely in tawny yellows, Réthymnon's old quarter is as picturesque as that of Chaniá. Venetians and Turks built their homes, churches, and mosques here, along with a solid, extensive system of fortifications – meant to be the 'town within a town' – on the hill that juts into the sea. The narrow streets, crowded with shops and restaurants, still bustle with activity.

Up until the 14th century, Réthymnon was no more than a tiny fishing hamlet but, by the beginning of the 16th century, it had grown into a significant town with a population of 10,000. The Greek and Venetian aristocracies divided up the power among themselves. Yet the common citizenry here, having acquired wealth from the burgeoning export trade, gained political influence earlier than elsewhere in Europe. In the outlying villages, however, the peasants were burdened with high taxes, and forced to contribute

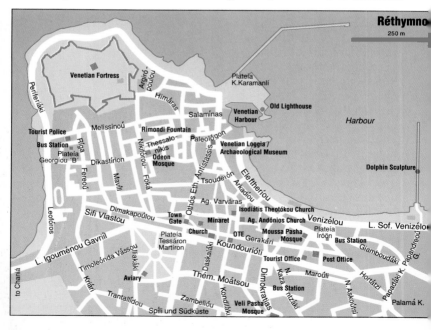

The old harbour of Réthymnon

their labour to erect the town's fortifications.

The Cretan Renaissance flowered at a time when Greece was already under Ottoman domination, but ushered in a unique period of literary excellence in Réthymnon. Yiórgios Chortátzis wrote his masterpiece, the tragedy *Erofíli*, during this period. In 1561, the first Greek intellectual centre since the days of Byzantium was founded here: the Vívi Academy. Kalliróï Párren-Siganú, the fore-runner of the Greek women's movement, was born in Réthymnon in 1856. All of this cultural ferment contributed to the town's reputation as a place of scholarship.

Today, Réthymnon is still the capital, trade centre and port of the Nomós of the same name. It is the smallest and most mountainous of Crete's prefectures – dominated by the Psilorítis massif – and the main agricultural products are olives, olive oil, carob and vegetables. Tourism, however, is beginning to play an increasingly important role, with approximately half of the 20,000 inhabitants drawing their income from the industry.

The Old Quarter with Fortézza

Réthymnon's Old Quarter

A tour of the town, its mosques and churches, streets and alleys full of shops and charming houses; a relaxing stop in one of the typical old 'kafeneía'.

The starting point for this walk through the town is the elongated central **Plateía Tessáron Martíron**. In 1824, three members of the Cretan aristocracy were executed here. They had been found guilty of the crime of remaining secret Christians despite their public conversion to Islam. The square is named after these martyrs and there is a popular festival held here in their honour every 28 October. A bronze monument commemorates another hero: Kostís Giamboudákis, who detonated the ammunition dump inside the Arkádi Monastery. Besieged by the Turks, over 1,000 people sheltering within chose death before dishonour. Towering above the square, you will see the minaret of the **Megáli Pórta Mosque**, which is entirely surrounded by buildings and can only be visited by way of the garden at Odós Tombási 27. The **Megáli Pórta**, also called Pórta Guora, is all that remains of the Venetian town wall built to protect Réthymnon from the south. It was the central town gate and is still the entrance to the Old Quarter.

This is where the **Odós Ethnikís Antístassis** begins, a street lined with shops, as well as with Venetian and Turkish houses, which are

Réthymnon's lighthouse

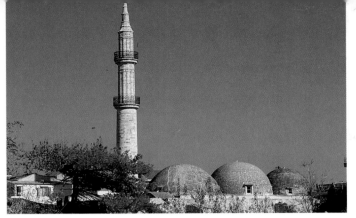

Neratsé Mosque

all worth long, leisurely examination. On the left-hand side, diagonally opposite the Odós Tsouderón and set back a bit from the
street, you will discover one of the most beautiful Venetian churches
on Crete: the renovated **San Francesco**, dating back to the
16th–17th century. Once the heart of an important monastery complex, it is today owned by the University of Crete and used for
public events. In the **Plateía Peticháki**, the former **Neratsé Mosque**,
largest of the five mosques still standing of the original eight, has
also been converted for secular use. The top of this minaret affords
visitors a marvellous view, out over the roofs of the Old Quarter to
the Fortézza in the north; along the extensive tourist beach in the
east; all the way to the Psilorítis and the Ida Mountains, in the
south-east. The mosque, formerly the Santa Anna Church and
topped by three cupolas, is used as a concert hall and music school
today. The Venetian **Rimondi Fountain**, installed further down on
the square in 1629, virtually disappears among the many tables and
chairs of the surrounding restaurants and cafés during summer. The
water gushes from four lions' heads between four slender columns
capped with Corinthian capitals. The Turkish dome-shaped roof
was partially destroyed during World War II.

Continuing up the hill, you will come to the Venetian **Fortézza**
on the rocky cape in the north, once the site of the ancient city of
Ríthimna. The cornerstone for
this complex of fortifications was
laid in 1573, and the battlements
were completed in 1580, the
fruits of some 76,800 days of
slave labour on the part of
the population. The fortress
proved too small to accom-
modate the entire populace
as was originally intended
and, in 1646, it withstood
the Turkish siege for only
30 days. The Turks
turned the episcopal

Megáli Pórta Mosque

seat into the Sultan Ibrahim Mosque, and it was here that the German Wehrmacht established a place of execution during World War II. Today, in summer, plays are performed and concerts held on one of the bastions facing the town. The former prison below the fortress houses the **Archaeological Museum**, which provides generous and attractive exhibition space for finds dating from the Neolithic to the Byzantine era; Late Minoan clay sarcophagi, ceramics, jewellery and coins. There is also a small **Folklore Museum** (Odós Messolongíou 28) opposite the Catholic Church.

It is now time to head for the harbour, built by the Venetians during the 13th century, walking along **Odós Paleóglou**, past the **Venetian Loggia**, once the gathering place of the Venetian aristocracy. The harbour has been rebuilt repeatedly and, in 1882, a canal was dug to prevent silting due to northerly winds and sea currents. Older residents can still remember waves lapping up against the restaurants on the seaside promenade. On summer evenings, the Old Harbour resembles one enormous dining room: one seafood restaurant follows another, punctuated by a small bar here and there, candles illuminating the tables and the diners' faces. At the other end of the seaside promenade, near the Plateía

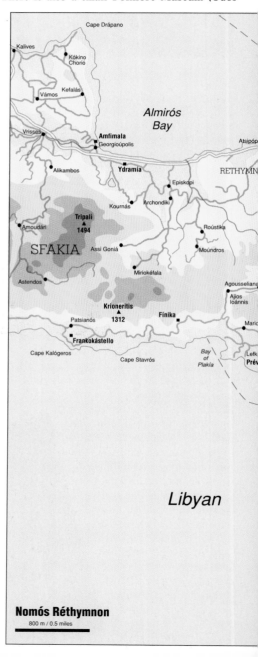

Nomós Réthymnon

800 m / 0.5 miles

Iróön, is the **Moussa Pasha Mosque**, only the stump of its minaret remaining, which houses the Monument Preservation Board. Above the bus terminal, is the **Véli Pasha Mosque** with its minaret, the former heart of a *teké*, or Islamic monastery, of which 13 cells have been preserved. The annual wine festival is held each July in the municipal park laid out during the 1920s near the **Megáli Pórta**. Across the street, on **Odós Kountouriói**, you will find refreshments at one of the typical old *kafeneía*.

TOUR 8

The Amári Basin

Take a hike, if you so desire, through this lovely terrain with its cherry, apple and olive trees; stop to inspect a monastery church; end the day with a trout dinner. A full day's excursion.

During the Venetian-Turkish War, the bard Bunialís of Réthymnon sang the praises of a hilly landscape surrounded by mountains – the Amári Basin – calling it 'Paradise', and Mt Kédros (1,777m/5,830ft), at its western edge the 'site of 100 springs'.

Flanked by Mt Psilorítis to the east, the **Amári Basin** stretches 25km (15½ miles) to the south, with 40 villages on its slopes, 4–500m (1,300–1,600ft) high. The basin is divided by **Mt Sámitos** (1,014m/3,327ft). Amári fruit is often praised, particularly the cherries and apples which thrive here, but also the table olives. This is the loveliest region on Crete and the most abundant in water. You would need days to visit all the tiny Byzantine churches scattered across the landscape – marvellous country for hikers.

The first stop on the main road is the **Church of Panaghía Myr-tiótiss**a in Prasiés, with remains of frescoes dating back to the 14th century. There are still a few Venetian houses extant in the village – evidence of former affluence. To the east, Prasiés Ravine stretches southward, and the green 'paradise' spreads out beyond the pass.

Beyond **Apóstoli** the road divides, the two forks circling opposite sides of the basin. To the south-west lies the large, scenic mountain village of **Méronas** which, back in 1878, was the seat of the revolutionary general assembly. Further up the mountain is the triple-naved **Panagheía Basilica** – its 14th-century frescoes only partially uncovered. Dating back to the 15th century, when painted panels began replacing frescoes, the wooden icon in the **Panagheía Odigí-tria** is one of the oldest on Crete. The road now winds its way to **Elenes** and the cherry-growing village of **Gerakári**, the starting

Apóstoli in the Amári Basin

point of an optional hike up **Mt Kédros**. The road to Ano and Káto Méros takes you down the **Platys river valley**. Here, the triple-arched Venetian bridge has remained standing next to its modern replacement.

Continuing towards the south-east, the next stop on your itinerary is the monastery church of **Valsamónerou**, 3km (1.9 miles) south of Vorízia. The monastery church contains frescoes which span several centuries – some of the most significant works of Byzantine art on Crete. The church is consecrated to Saint Phanoúrious, among others, a patron saint of lost objects or causes. To gain admission to the church, ask in Vorízia ('Pou íneh o filakas tou monastiríou?' – 'Where is the caretaker of the monastery?').

A bit further south, 3km (1.9 miles) this side of Zarós, watch for the next monastery on the southern slope of Mt Psilorítis. **Moní Vrontíssi** (550m/1,804ft), surrounded by mighty, sentinel-like 2,000-year-old plane trees, was first documented in the year 1400. In the double-naved church in the middle of the spacious courtyard, you can admire the beautifully restored 14th-century frescoes and wooden icons which come from Valsamónerou Monastery.

Zarós, a large, green mountain village further south, at the foot of Mt Psilorítis, is known for its trout farms. Here you should dine at one of the trout restaurants situated above the town. The road heads back north via **Kamáres**, a point of departure for hikes in the Psilorítis range, to **Vizári**. A gravel road opposite the post office takes you to the well-preserved foundations of the former **episcopal basilica**, which dates from the 7th century. According to legend, this is where, until 1821, Antifandís – a participant in Napoleon's Egyptian campaign – trained the troops so dreaded by the Turks.

The stretch of road into the one-time 'capital' of **Amári** is lined with pines, Eucalyptus trees and grain fields. A walk up to the cemetery is worth the spectacular view of Psilorítis. At the entrance to the village some young people have opened a pretty restaurant which serves very good food. Before returning to Réthymnon, take one last detour to the hamlet of **Thrónos**: the mosaics of the former episcopal basilica located in front of the small, single-naved **Church of the Panagheía Throniótissa** (with its 15th-century frescoes) bear witness to its days as a diocesan town.

47

Préveli Monastery and Frankokástello

A Late Minoan necropolis; Préveli Monastery; Fort Franko-kástello, with its inexplicable 'shadow warriors'; and a refreshing swim. A full day's excursion.

Your route today consists almost entirely of well-maintained roads, and you will have plenty of time for some leisurely bathing along your way. Ten kilometres (6 miles) south of Réthymnon, just before reaching the village of **Arméni**, situated in the middle of a grove of oak trees is a **Late Minoan necropolis**, one of the largest such burial sites in Europe. A shepherd discovered the first grave here in the late 1960s; today, 64 rock chambers have been excavated, containing sarcophagi, earthenware, jewellery, tools and seals.

Twenty-three kilometres (14 miles) out of Réthymnon on the main road to Aghia Galíni, there is a fork to the right, to the monastery of Moní Préveli, which leads through one of the most beautiful ravines in the Léfka Ori, **Kourtaliótiko Gorge**. The north wind blows here, frequently and fiercely, producing the rattling sound – *koúrtala* – for which the area is named. The stream flowing through the ravine is the **Megalopótamos**. Popular tradition attributes the origins of the springs from which it flows to Saint Nikólaos who, like Moses, caused water to gush forth from stones.

After leaving the canyon and before beginning to climb, the road comes to an old, arched stone bridge, surrounded by rushes and osiers, which spans a river which flows all year long, emptying into the sea further south. It is worth the brief climb to explore the 16th–17th-century **Káto Monastery** (consecrated to John the Baptist) further up the hill. The road continues to climb to the **Préveli Monastery** which dates back to the 17th century. 'It is the paradise of Crete,' wrote the English cartographer Spratt during the last century, 'at an extremely happily selected site conducive to withdrawing from the cares and responsibilities of life.'

Préveli Monastery

The monastery's affluence was based on those classical treasures of Crete – olives, honey, and flocks of goats and sheep. Many Orthodox Christians bequeathed their possessions to the monastery to prevent them from falling into the hands of the Turks – so that its vast estates eventually reached from the Libyan to the Cretan Sea. During World War II it was from here that Allied soldiers were evacuated to Egypt, after which the Germans looted the monastery. Only the silver cross containing the splinter of the True

Káto Préveli Monastery

Cross was returned, because the German aircraft with this precious freight on board was simply unable to get off the ground. Nearly all of the 20 cells here are unoccupied today: this lovely monastery with its view over the southern sea has become, for the most part, a sightseers' destination. Annually, on 8 May, the church's patron saint, Ioánnis O Theológos (John the Evangelist), is honoured. Once, the festivities called for the sacrifice of cattle, a holdover from the rites of antiquity.

Through a harsh, karstic landscape – rarely charming, almost chilly – high above the southern coast, the road continues through the villages of Káto and Ano Rodákino (Lower and Upper Peach), down onto the plain to **Fort Frankokástello** located directly on the sea where there is a long stretch of flat sandy beach and several *tavérnes*. Built by the Venetians in 1371 as a refuge for the local population, the fort was also used against the resistance fighter Sfakiás. The rectangular outer walls with their towers at each corner are still standing. In 1828, 700 freedom fighters lost their lives here. The monument erected to commemorate their heroism is dedicated to their general, Hadzimihális. No adequate scientific explanation has ever been found for a mysterious phenomenon involving the phantoms or ghosts of these warriors, the *drossoulítes,* or 'dew men' which appear in the first light of dawn here in the latter half of May. The mirage occurs only when atmospheric conditions are ideal, when an army of soldiers appears out of the mist.

Just beyond the fort is the Byzantine church of **Aghios Nikítas** with its 14th-century frescoes, built on the foundations of an early Christian basilica. Below the building, at the foot of a bluff, there is another sandy beach, and it only remains to say '*Kaló bányo*', or 'Have a good swim'.

Fort Frankokástello

The Soul of Crete

Argiroúpolis, a large mountain village among cypresses and olive trees; the high Kalikrátis Plateau; dinner at a cosy tavérna. A half day's trip.

The old road from Réthymnon to Chaniá threads its way through a silvery landscape blanketed with olive trees, and hamlets off the beaten track. This side of **Episkopí**, the road bends southward and begins to climb. Only 260m (853ft) above the sea and not far from it, lies the former silver mining town, **Argiroúpolis**, a large mountain village on the site of the ancient settlement of Láppa. Once a mighty city of 10,000 people, Láppa experienced its heyday when Crete was a Roman province. Today, you can pick out ruined fragments of Láppa's structures incorporated into the walls of houses or scattered in front of churches. During Minoan times, all of Crete must have been forested as densely as the environs of Agiroúpolis. The Venetian church belfries are the last reminders of the days when the town was still an important centre of Venetian Crete. During the Turkish era, its status declined to that of a *gaïthourópolis*, or 'Donkey Town'. But at an assembly in 1878 this town is where the question of union with Greece was resolved.

Further south, higher up the mountain, lies tiny **Myriokéfala** — its new church of the **Panagheía Odigítria** containing parts of the old church and marvellous frescoes dating back to the 11th–12th centuries. The interior of the church resembles a defensive fortress. On 7 and 8 September, as many as 15,000 people throng here to the festivities honouring the Virgin.

View of Argiroúpolis

A quiet spot in Argiroúpolis

From here, double back, past strawberry patches, to the lush green valley below Argiroúpolis, irrigated by the same cataract which supplies Réthymnon with drinking water. The plane trees, particularly tall here, banana groves, poplars, and nut and fig trees – and, especially, the water – make this place a popular destination for summer outings. Try the *tavérna* (closed in winter) directly beside one of the streams for a bite to eat.

The next stretch of your journey passes through **Gyparis Gulch** to **Asigoniá**, as the Turks called the village: 'Revolutionaries' Nook'. The lyrics of a popular song run: 'I told you, Mother, I cannot bear the Turks and cannot be a slave. So give me my gun and my silver knife, so that I can go to Asigoniá…' It is a large village on a mountainside dotted with walnut trees and home to many flocks of sheep. On St George's Day, 23 April or, when Orthodox Easter comes late, on the following Tuesday, the shepherds drive their sheep into the village, where the animals are blessed, milked, and the milk distributed to the people.

The 12km (7.5 miles) of bad gravel road leading from here up to the small **Plateau of Kallikrátis** (760m/2,522ft) may be a bit tedious, but what magic once you reach the top. The soul of Crete is surely its mountains, and those who inhabit the peaks! Of the 400 families which used to live up here – except in winter – only 80 remain. There are a few *kafeneía* where visitors will find a good meal. On 15 August, the village, whose men are considered the handsomest on the island, fills with people for a big *paniyíri*. During the winter, when the inhabitants move down to their winter quarters in Kapsodássos, Kallikrátis is totally deserted.

From here you can either retrace your steps or go via Episkopí to the small freshwater **Lake of Kournás**, or proceed via the gravel road to Adkífou and Vrísses. In the village of **Kournás** – not located on the lake – there is a small *tavérna* on the main road (on the side towards the lake), where you will find hearty, delicious food. During the winter, the place is particulary cosy with its roaring, iron stove. From the resort of Georgioúpolis, take the national highway and go back, or on, to Chaniá.

The Lake of Kournás

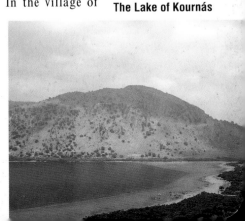

Margarítes and Arkádi

The potters' village of Margarítes and the legendary Monastery of Arkádi. A half day's excursion.

The first stop on the way to the south-east is at the **Arsaníou Monastery**, above the coast and 6km (3¾ miles) from Réthymnon. Inhabited by only a couple of monks, it is like so many Greek monasteries. Destroyed many times throughout history, there is little left here except a few beautiful icons in the monastery museum. An old drawing gives an impression of how spacious the monastery complex must once have been. The ancient city of Agrion is believed to have been located near here.

In Cháni Alexándrou, located on the old road to Irákleion, the road forks off to **Margarítes**, one of Crete's four historic pottery centres. It was from here that the master craftsmen, all organised into guilds, used to swarm out over the island during the summer, producing their wares in the towns along their way. In 1928 half the population still lived off the production of unglazed pottery. Legend tells of a queen in the ancient city of Eléftherna nearby, who was so enchanted by the location of the town that she donated her jewellery towards the founding of the village. Above the village, you can still inspect the remains of the old firing kilns. Young potters are now hoping to carry on the ancient traditions.

The monastery church of Arkádi

Arkádi Monastery

The road continues up the mountain to **Eléftherna** gloriously perched on a jutting nose of rock. The most striking remains are the 6m (20ft) high cisterns. Along with Láppa, Eléftherna was one of the mightiest cities in the Roman province of Crete. From Eléftherna, the next stretch of road – only half of it paved and rarely marked on road maps – takes you to the most legendary of all Cretan monasteries, **Moní Arkádi**. At an elevation of 500m (1,640ft), the monastery is located 23km (14 miles) south-west of Réthymnon amidst grain fields and tall pines. The Venetian-Cretan stone façade displays the full palette of Mediterranean colours: pink, delicate yellow, beige and ochre.

On 9 November 1866, after a brutal day of fighting against the 150,000 Ottoman soldiers who were besieging the monastery, the 1,000 Orthodox Christians within the walls, unwilling to submit to the Turks, blew themselves up. There were 114 survivors, and the Ottoman casualties numbered 1,500 dead or wounded. As a result of the Arkádi tragedy, funds were raised throughout Europe in support of the Cretan struggle. The monastery that stands at Arkádi today was erected in the 16th–17th century, the façade of the main church one of the most beautiful on the island.

Potter in Margarítes

The road by way of Amnátos, Chamalévri and Stavroménos takes you back to the national highway.

Mount Ida, Zeus's Birthplace

Churches, shepherds and sheep; the cave where Zeus was born. A half day's outing.

From Réthymnon, follow the old road via Plataniás and Pérama, climbing to an elevation of 510m (1,673ft), to Axós at the northern foot of the Psilorítis range. In Minoan times, **Axós** was where one spent the night when travelling from eastern to western Crete. Today, it is a destination on the itineraries of tourists in coaches or private cars driving to Anóghia and the Ida Cave on the Nída Plateau. With all the shops here selling the usual tourist tat, it is hard to believe that this is where the Minoans retreated in order to escape the advancing hordes of Dorians. Later, the Dorians took the city anyway, fortified it and built an acropolis a bit further up. Axós remained a wealthy and powerful town up until Byzantine times, when the population moved and founded Anóghia.

At a fork in the road in the middle of town you will discover the beautiful **Aghía Iríni Church**, with its groin-vaulted cupola and 14th–15th-century frescoes. The frescoes dating from the same period are worth seeing in the **Aghios Ioánnis Church** located in the cemetery at the eastern end of the village. Despite the numbers of visitors, the large, populous village of **Anóghia** is still a beautiful place, known throughout Greece for its fine musicians. The *lyra* player and singer Psarantónis, brother of the widely revered singer, Níkos Xiloúris, who died in 1980, and Ludivíkos, whose repertoire consists of old love songs and laments from his village, are both native Anóghians.

Anóghia has a heroic history of rebellion as well. Destroyed twice by the Turks, in 1821 and 1866, Anóghia was razed to the ground and all its men executed by the Germans in 1944. Due to its remote location, Greek traditions and age-old customs are exceptionally well preserved here, along with a distinctive, Dorian dialect.

Located 21km (13 miles) from Anóghia, at an elevation of 1,400 metres (4,593ft), we reach the small, practically circular **Nída Plateau**. With an area of only four square kilometres (1½ square miles), it is populated by shepherds and thousands of sheep. The road, only half of it paved, makes its

Aghía Irini Church in Axós

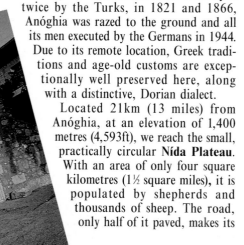

The Nída Plateau

way through the barren, mountainous terrain, past *mitáta* – the
shepherds' round, unplastered huts, which bear an interesting re-
semblance to Minoan burial vaults – and *stroúnga*, round walled-in
places where the sheep are milked and shorn.

There have been inns and *tavérnes* on the plateau since the Bronze
Age, serving the pilgrims drawn to the nearby **Ida Cave** – which
was a place of worship from the Stone Age well into the early
Christian era. This cave on the northern flank of Mt Psilorítis is located in almost exactly the centre of Crete. What is more, this is the
cave where Zeus, the father of the Greek gods, was believed to have
been born. Every nine years, the great King Mínos came here to receive from the god himself the laws and regulations which provided
the foundation for Mínos's wise rule. Today, developers are thinking
of promoting winter sports activities here, and on the Omálos
Plateau in Nomós Chaniá.

From Anóghia, continue along the old road to Irákleion, visiting
the remains of three Minoan manor houses in **Tílissos** on the way.

Inside the Melídoni Cave near Pérama

IRÁKLEION

Irákleion is the largest and most important city, economically, on Crete. With over a fifth of the island's population living here in what is the fourth largest city in Greece, Irákleion is rapidly turning into an urban jungle, the 'Athens of Crete', as detractors call it. Besides becoming the Cretan capital in 1972, Irákleion is also the administrative capital and the trade centre for the seven districts of the Nomós. Irákleion has a population of 120,000. This is where most of the charter flights land, and the majority of the now over one million summer visitors stop off here at least once during their stay.

All this crowding produces quite a hustle and bustle, especially in summer. But Irákleion lacks the Venetian-Turkish flair of Chaniá or Réthymnon and has far fewer beautiful old buildings. Despite its shortcomings however, Irákleion is a city with a certain cosmopolitan dash, a trading city with a long tradition. The growth in tourism since the 1970s has given rise to a renovation program for the old quarter of town but, unfortunately, very little of historical value has been left standing.

Irákleion's past is as turbulent as that of Crete. Under the Arabs, Rabdh el-Khandak, as they called it, had the dubious distinction of containing the biggest pirates' lair and slave market in the Eastern Mediterranean. In the process of recapturing Crete for Byzantium, Nikifóros Fokás, at the head of the siege force, had the heads of

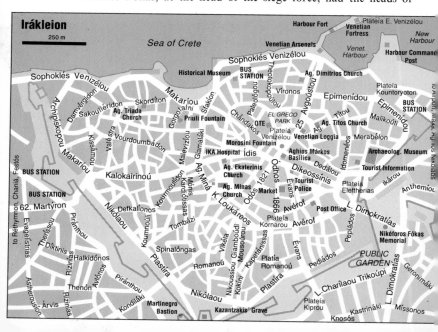

Irákleion harbour

prisoners catapulted into the beleaguered city. Finally, in 961, he razed the city to the ground, had the Arab population killed or enslaved, bestowing upon what was left of the town the name 'Chántaka'. After a brief Genoese interlude on Crete, the Venetians finally seized the island in 1210, turning 'Chántaka' into 'Candia', and frequently calling the entire island the 'Isola di Candia'. In the 15th century, the school of painting belonging to the monastery of Aghía Ekateríni of Mount Sinai developed into a sort of university, becoming the intellectual centre of the island and flagship of the Cretan Renaissance in general.

In the streets of Irákleion

During the 16th century, the mightiest fortifications in the Mediterranean were built around Candia. In 1699, after a 22-year siege, Turks marched into the city. One final cataclysm in the saga of Greek resistance, on 25 August 1898, caused the major powers to declare Crete's autonomy. World War II ended seven months earlier in Irákleion than on the west of the island, thanks to the cunning of 50 partisans who managed to trick the enemy into believing they were a superior force numbering in their thousands.

Walking through 'Candia'

A tour of Irákleion's Old Quarter covering the the Arab and Byzantine city of Candia: the Aghios Márkos Basilica, Venetian fort, Rocca del Mare and Archaeological Museum.

Plateía E Venizélou, in the heart of the city, is a good starting point for this tour of the town. With its numerous cafés and restaurants, it is a popular meeting place, and not only for Irákleion's foreign guests. Once the grain market, today the square is a pedestrian zone. The beautiful Venetian **Morosini Fountain**, with its four water-spouting lions, presented to the public in 1628, is the symbol of the city. An **Aqueduct**, over 15km (9 miles) long, was meant to provide Candia with water from Arhánes. The reliefs on the outer walls depict stories from ancient Greek mythology, including Zeus's abduction of the Phoenician king's daughter,

Theotokópoulos Exhibition in the Aghios Márkos Basilica

Europa. The church with three naves across the way is the **Aghios Márkos Basilica**, the former San Marco's, consecrated in 1239 and the seat of the Latin bishops during the Venetian occupation. Under the crescent moon of Islam, the church was converted into the Defterdar Mosque and its campanile torn down. The beautiful interior, with its wood-panelled naves, is a venue for city cultural events today. In 1990, it hosted the first exhibition on the island of works by Crete's most famous painter, Doménikos Theotokópoulos, better known as El Greco.

The centre of social activity in Candia was the loggia on **Odós 25 Avgoústou** (25 August Street). After its destruction by earthquake, the building remained a ruin until the end of the World War II. Today, it is Irákleion's city hall. The Street of 25 August – the site of the last Cretan bloodshed at the hands of the Turks – leads to the Venetian harbour, and has long been the city's main social and commercial artery. Most of Irákleion's streets are now dominated by modern buildings, but there are still enough old façades to convey a hint of the city's former splendour. Today, despite its rich history, the street is characterised by banks, ship-

ping and travel agencies, and the ubiquitous souvenir shops. Not far from Aghios Márkos, situated in a small square, the **Aghios Títos Church** served believers of several faiths before becoming an Orthodox sanctuary in 1924. The skull of Saint Títos (Titus) was returned here in 1966 from its sojourn in Venice.

The Venetian harbour of Irákleion lacks the unity and charm of the harbours of Chaniá and Réthymnon. Located directly on the heavily-travelled shoreline drive, it is a mooring place for fishing boats. The only thing left to remind you of the days of Venetian and Byzantine glory is the renovated fort, **Rocca del Mare**, which has retained its Turkish name, 'Kúles', and is one of the most beautiful Venetian forts in the Mediterranean. The open upper floor, with its stump of a minaret, is the summer venue of dramatic performances and concerts. A walk along the mole is certainly worthwhile, though not many of the former Venetian arsenals, where galleys were overhauled in the winter, ships built and merchandise stored, have been left standing. Inside the old city wall, **Odós Doukós** leads up to **Plateía Eleftherías**. Until 1917, the eastern city gate, Aghios Geórgios, was located here – also called Lazaréto, because the street to the 'plague house' passed through it.

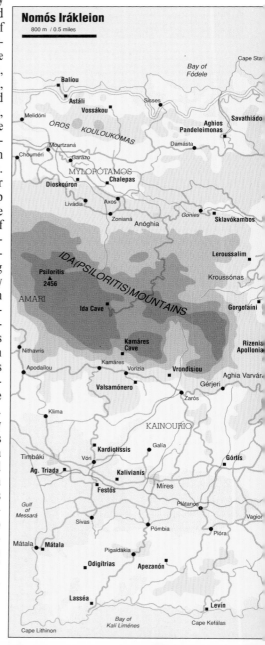

Nomós Irákleion

800 m / 0.5 miles

Today, the gate has been replaced with a bust of Irákleion's great literary lion, Níkos Kazantzákis, author of *Zorba the Greek, Report to Greco* and *The Last Temptation of Christ*.

One place you must allow plenty of time for is the **Archaeological Museum**, founded in 1878. Covering two floors are the spectacular finds from 5,500 years of rich Cretan history; particularly notable, those from the Minoan excavations. To gain an understanding of Minoan culture, there is no substitute for a visit to this museum.

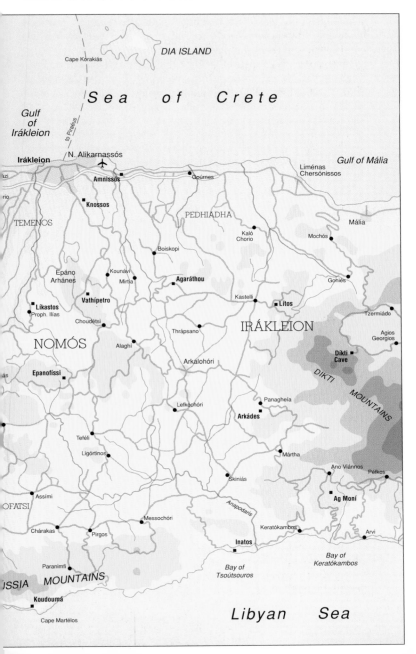

Venetian Ramparts

The quarter in which the Venetians built their palaces; the view from the 'Slumbering Zeus'; the impressive fortress of Michele Sanmicheli; churches and museums.

To Cretans, **Mt Yoúchtas** (811m/2,661ft), to the south of Irákleion, looks like a slumbering Zeus, reclining in full battle gear, his helmet and profile silhouetted against the sky. At the southern point of the fortification walls of the Martinengo Bastion – jutting into the countryside like an enormous triangle – you will find the grave of Níkos Kazantzákis, probably Greece's best known author. The epitaph under the simple wooden cross was written by the novelist, and mirrors his philosophy. Strangely reminiscent of WB Yeats's epitaph, it reads: 'I hope for nothing, I fear nothing, I am free.'

The inspiring view from this impressive vantage point should put

Turkish pump house in Irákleion

you in the right frame of mind to begin your second tour of Irákleion. Turning your back on the 'Slumbering Zeus', you will be looking out over the fortress wall of **Michele Sanmicheli**, right on the edge of the growing city of New Irákleion. Over 3km (1.9 miles) long and up to 60m (65yds) thick, it encloses an area of around 800m^2 (957 square yards). All the men from the surrounding area between the ages of 14 and 60 were enlisted for one week of compulsory labour per year in the building of the fortress. The bastions, housing artillery casements, consisted of several storeys, all connected by tunnels 15–20m (50–65ft) deep. The old access points to the city – the Pórta Chanión to the west, the Komméno Benténi to the south-west, the Kenoúria Pórta to the south-east and the Tris Kamáres to the east – are still in use, although not all of the city gates are still standing.

Plateía Kornárou is the setting not only of the oldest existing Venetian fountain (executed by Zuanne Bambo, with a headless Ro-

The two churches of Aghios Minás

man statue from Ierápetra) and the Turkish pump house – which is used as a *kafeneíon* today – but, since 1981, also of the sculpture of Erotókritos and Aretoússa, the star-crossed lovers of the Cretan national epic, *Erotókritos,* which was written by Vitséntzos Kornáros.

From the square proceed directly to the bazaar, located in **Odós 1866**, the street whose name commemorates the uprising at the Arkádi Monastery. If you are hungry, look for *tavérnes* and hot food stalls in the side streets off the bazaar. The former church of **Aghía Ekateríni** on **Plateía Aghía Ekateríni** belonged to the famous **St Catharine's Monastery** on Mount Sinai, and was once the heart of the Cretan Renaissance movement. This austere building, with its barrel vaulting and cuppola, a mixture of Venetian and Islamic architecture, is almost completely preserved. Today it houses the **Icon Museum**. The most important holdings here are the panels executed by Michaïl Damaskinós.

In the same square, unofficially known as the Square of Churches, you will also find the relatively new **Aghios Minás Church**, tangible proof of the continuity of Greek sacred architecture. Completed in 1895, as the archiepiscopal cathedral, it accommodates 8,000 people. Crete has had its own archbishop since 1967, directly responsible to the Greek Orthodox Patriarch in Constantinople. The **Little Aghios Minás Church**, a two-room chapel dating back to the 15th–16th century, is tiny and modest by comparison, but lavishly furnished with a marvellous iconostasis, and picture-panelled walls with typical Cretan carvings and icons by Geórgios Kastrofílakas.

West of the harbour, your next stop is the **Historical and Folklore Museum**. The exhibits document the more recent chapters in the city's history: the library and study of Níkos Kazantzákis, photographs of the Battle of Crete, and of the battle-scarred city of Irákleion, prints of old Candia, traditional costumes, woven articles, etc. Foot-weary and hungry, you may now want to cross little **El Greco Park** to reach **Plateía Venizélou**, where several restaurants provide a respite from all this culture-consumption.

Potters and Mountain Villages

A day trip in the environs of Irákleion; a potters' village; market day in a mountain village; relaxing under shady plane trees. A full day tour.

Throughout Crete, if you drive into the more remote regions you will find winding roads, often of poor quality, and no infrastructure of tourist services. Twenty-three kilometres (14 miles) south of Irákleion, you will come to the **Monastery (Moni) of Angaráthou**. At an elevation of nearly 400m (1,312ft), idyllically situated above hills covered with vineyards, this is one of the oldest monasteries on Crete. It played an important role both in the struggle against the Turks and as a centre of intellectual activity. In former times, there was always water, wine, bread and olives deposited in a niche in the flower-filled courtyard, ready to be served to visiting travellers. Today, this tradition continues in the *trápeza,* or refectory. The church possesses a 'miraculous' icon of John the Baptist. During a Turkish attack in 1896, the bullets of a Turkish soldier bounced off it, blinding the man; smoke and noise filled the air and the Turks took to their heels. That, at least, is how the monks tell the story.

After looping around via Vóni, you will arrive in the village of **Thrápsano**, the pottery centre of the Nomós Irákleion. As late as the 1960s, Thrápsano potters organised in guilds fanned out from here to other parts of the island – mainly to fire the characteristic, man-sized storage vessels, or *píthi*, used in Minoan times. In the intervening decades, however, the potters have settled down, and their *píthi*, rarely used now to store oil and wine, serve mainly as giant planters. In addition to the village's several small workshops, there is a potters' co-operative south of town from which the terracotta ceramics – still turned by hand as they have been for thousands of years – are exported throughout Europe.

From here it is not far to **Kastélli/Pediáda**. Despite its proximity to the tourist 'strongholds' of Chersónissos, Amnissós and Mália, this has remained a sleepy little one-mule town. Just a stone's throw away, above the village of Xidás, keep your

The pottery in Thrapsanó

The area around the Epanosífi Monastery

eyes open for a narrow track through the fields. There isn't so much as a sign to indicate that this was once the location of Lyttos, one of the mightiest cities of ancient Crete, its port being present-day Chersónissos. The excavations are modest, but the location on the north-western slope of the Díkti Mountain range and the view are spectacular. Due to its protected location, Lyttos was not fortified – a rarity, and a luxury in the bellicose ancient world.

The agricultural centre of the area is the large mountain village of **Arkalohóri**, south-west of Kastélli. Here, Saturday is market day, and the place bustles with people buying merchandise. Arkalohóri's reputation is based on the Minoan findings discovered here in 1932 in the Profítis Ilías Cave. According to the late archaeologist Spyridon Marinátos, there is reason to believe that this is the original Díkti Cave, the reputed 'birthplace' of Zeus.

In the beautiful old mountain village of **Ano Viánnos** on the road to Ierápetra, you can soak up pure village atmosphere sitting outside a *kafeneíon* under 220-year-old plane trees. This is where Ioánnis Kondilákis was born in 1861. His novel *Patoúchas* captures with great charm the way of life in a Cretan village. Outside the town, look for a simple monument to the 400 men, women, and children from surrounding villages shot and set afire here in 1943 by German soldiers. Down below, beside the Bay of Keratókambos, is the small village of **Arvis**, famous for its small, fragrant bananas.

The road now heads north via Pírgos on the edge of the Messará Plain to the **Epanosífi Monastery**, still home to 30 monks. It is a so-called idiorrhythmic monastery, where each monk keeps house for himself and property is private rather than communal. In front of the church, the large stone table surrounded by stone benches is where the first wine casks are opened and the first *tsigouthiá* tasted every 3 November, at the religious festival honouring Saint George.

The wine-growers' association in the otherwise nondescript village of **Pezá** on the way back to Irákleion produces some of the finest wine on the island.

Arhánes, Vathípetro and Mt Yoúchtas

A small town worth visiting not only for its Minoan excavations; a Minoan wine-growing estate with a marvellous view; up Mt Yoúchtas to the birthplace of Cretan Zeus. A half day tour.

At the foot of **Mt Yoúchtas**, in the middle of Crete's richest wine-growing region, you will find the cheerful town of **Arhánes**, which has managed to preserve its authentic character even though Irákleion is only 15km (9 miles) away.

The town gleams – with its *arhontiká spitia* (manor houses), its beautiful old *kafeneía* with their high windows, and its covered sidewalks, all radiating bourgeois affluence. With its three naves and detached bell tower, the Venetian **Panagheía Church** on the main street is worth seeing. Irákleionites enjoy driving out in the evening with their *paréa* (close friends) for dinner. Who knows – the *tavérna* keeper may be serving ambrosia and nectar here, instead of more contemporary fare? Arhánes became internationally famous as a result of excavations which proved the site was the location of a major centre of Minoan culture. The complex unearthed in the former Turkish Quarter, the *tourkoyitoniá*, indicates that it was quite a splendid town in antiquity (to the left of the main road as you enter the town from Irákleion).

The **Fourní Necropolis** is difficult to find, so you should seek out the *filakas,* or caretaker, at one of the *kafeneía*. The necropolis is where a truly sensational find was made: the unplundered grave of

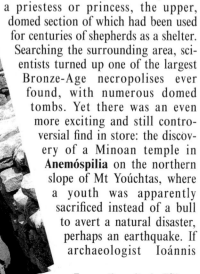

a priestess or princess, the upper, domed section of which had been used for centuries of shepherds as a shelter. Searching the surrounding area, scientists turned up one of the largest Bronze-Age necropolises ever found, with numerous domed tombs. Yet there was an even more exciting and still controversial find in store: the discovery of a Minoan temple in **Anemóspilia** on the northern slope of Mt Yoúchtas, where a youth was apparently sacrificed instead of a bull to avert a natural disaster, perhaps an earthquake. If archaeologist Ioánnis

Excavation site in Tílissos

Wayside scene near Epanosífi

Sakellarákis' theories are correct, this represents the only such occurrence on Crete. Despite publication in such periodicals as *National Geographic*, the sacrifice is still in dispute.

The *fílakas* is also in charge of the Minoan wine-growing estate in **Vathípetro**, south of Arhánes – reached via a gravel road leading up and to the left after the turn-off to Yoúchtas. It is a small estate and its open terrain affords a magnificent view of the vine-covered, hilly landscape. The excavated sites include a wine press, a weaving shop and a pottery. Coming to the end of this tour, climb the gravel road to the mythical **Mt Yoúchtas** (811m/2,661ft), preferably on foot, if it is not too hot.

According to the myth, this is the location of the grave of Cretan Zeus who, unlike Olympian Zeus, was immortal, and annually resurrected from the dead. The **Summit Chapel**, to which people throng for a *paniyíri* on 6 August, is not consecrated to the prophet Elijah (who, like Zeus, is responsible for the weather) as is customary, but to the Transfiguration of Christ, *Metamórphosis Christoú*. After all, like Zeus, Christ died and rose again.

Knossós and Mália

An outing for archaeology enthusiasts. A half-day excursion.

Both Knossós and Mália are easy to reach by rural bus. The best season to visit the palaces, especially **Knossós**, is between November and March, when the busloads of visitors are absent.

The English historian Arthur Evans, who originally travelled to Crete in search of clay tablets etched with hieroglyphics, excavated an area of 20,000m² (23,920 square yards). In the years since, scholars have come to doubt Evans' assumption that Knossós was the location of King Minos's palace. It seems more likely that the site was a trade centre governed by a priestess-queen, although there will be no hard and fast evidence for this premise as long as the 'Minoan' script remains undeciphered. One thing is certain, however: the Greek archaeologist who first located the giant *píthi* here, Mínos Kalokerinós, and Evans, who reconstructed the site, did succeed in discovering the most important city of ancient Crete.

A model in the Archaeological Museum in Irákleion will give you a good idea of what things looked like here during the Late Palatial period, from 1600–1450BC. The two- to four-storey buildings were connected in irregular fashion and grouped around a large inner courtyard surrounded by open passageways, with red-painted cypress trunks as supports and large frescoes on the walls. Evans had parts of buildings and columns reconstructed out of re-

Unearthed amphorae

The Palace of Knossós

inforced concrete – which met with a great deal of criticism. Note the representation of the double axe and the bull's horns: the attributes of the Great Goddess, prevalent motifs in Asia Minor during the Late Stone Age and, in fact, as early as the Early Stone Age in Europe. An earlier palace here was destroyed by a natural disaster in 1700BC; the newer one in around 1450BC. Nevertheless, Knossós flourished during the Classical Period, remaining one of the island's major urban centres until the Roman era. In AD827, the Arabs dealt it its death blow.

The road to **Mália** – the second oldest ancient palace excavated on Crete – takes you through the oldest cultivated landscape in Europe. Mass tourism has taken its toll here. The most extreme example is **Chersónissos** with its fashionable shops, which becomes a ghost town in winter. East of the village of Mália lay the Minoan port town, grouped around an unfortified palace. The excavated complex here dates back to the Late Palatial Period. The architecture at Mália was much simpler than at Knóssos.

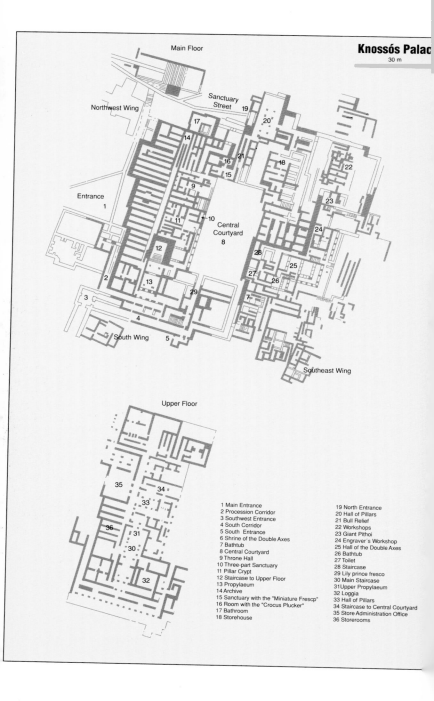

Main Floor

Knossós Palac

30 m

Sanctuary Street

Northwest Wing

Entrance

Central Courtyard
8

South Wing

Southeast Wing

Upper Floor

1 Main Entrance
2 Procession Corridor
3 Southwest Entrance
4 South Corridor
5 South Entrance
6 Shrine of the Double Axes
7 Bathtub
8 Central Courtyard
9 Throne Hall
10 Three-part Sanctuary
11 Pillar Crypt
12 Staircase to Upper Floor
13 Propylaeum
14 Archive
15 Sanctuary with the "Miniature Frescp"
16 Room with the "Crocus Plucker"
17 Bathroom
18 Storehouse

19 North Entrance
20 Hall of Pillars
21 Bull Relief
22 Workshops
23 Giant Pithoi
24 Engraver´s Workshop
25 Hall of the Double Axes
26 Bathtub
27 Toilet
28 Staircase
29 Lily prince fresco
30 Main Staircase
31 Upper Propylaeum
32 Loggia
33 Hall of Pillars
34 Staircase to Central Courtyard
35 Store Administration Office
36 Storerooms

A Roman Metropolis

From the centre of Crete to the agricultural Messará Plain: more ancient ruins, churches and palaces. A half-day excursion.

Just this side of **Aghía Varvára**, on the road to Míres and Festós, there is a small church perched on a rock. This is believed to mark the centre of Crete, the exact middle of the island. Once you have skirted the foothills of the Psilorítis range and climbed the **Vourvorlítis Pass**, you have a clear view of the **Messará Plain**. Forty kilometres (25 miles) long and 8–12km (5–7 miles) wide, and cut

The fertile Messará Plain

off from the sea by the **Asteroúsia Mountains** to the south, this is Crete's largest agricultural area. Here, too, you will find greenhouses popping up like mushrooms.

This side of Górtis, also called Górtina, you will come to the village of **Aghïï Théka**, named for 10 martyred bishops tortured to death here during the 3rd century. In the gorgeous quarter around the **Aghïï Théka Basilica**, dating back to the 13th–14th century, you may well come across the remains of the odd Roman column in the middle of the street.

71

Aghia Triátha

The ruins of the Roman capital of **Górtis** spread out on both sides of the road. Scholars inform us that it was once inhabited by 200,000 people, the most important city on the island for a good 1,000 years until it was devastated by the advancing Arabs during the 9th century. The fenced-in area to the north of the road contains the **ruins** of the Church of St Títos, once a mighty, domed basilica with three naves, as well as of the Agorá and the Market. The **stone tablets** along the northern wall of the Odeon document the acclaimed municipal laws of Górtis, which earned Crete the reputation in the ancient world of being particularly sophisticated in the realm of jurisprudence.

South of the road, in the middle of an olive grove, is centre of power, the **Praetorium**, the palace district of the Roman praetor. Like the remains of the Temple of Apollon Pythios, it is fenced in, but accessible to view. The excavations here draw considerably fewer visitors, which makes for a wonderfully quiet atmosphere.

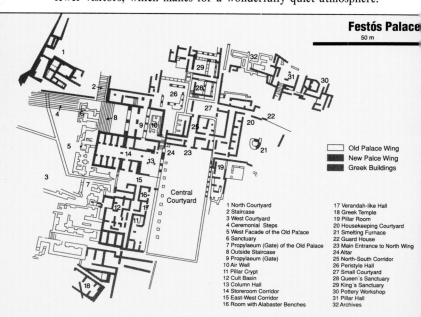

Festós Palace

50 m

Old Palace Wing
New Palce Wing
Greek Buildings

1 North Courtyard
2 Staircase
3 West Courtyard
4 Ceremonial Steps
5 West Facade of the Old Palace
6 Sanctuary
7 Propylaeum (Gate) of the Old Palace
8 Outside Staircase
9 Propylaeum (Gate)
10 Air Well
11 Pillar Crypt
12 Cult Basin
13 Column Hall
14 Storeroom Corridor
15 East-West Corridor
16 Room with Alabaster Benches
17 Verandah-like Hall
18 Greek Temple
19 Pillar Room
20 Housekeeping Courtyard
21 Smelting Furnace
22 Guard House
23 Main Entrance to North Wing
24 Altar
25 North-South Corridor
26 Peristyle Hall
27 Small Courtyard
28 Queen's Sanctuary
29 King's Sanctuary
30 Pottery Workshop
31 Pillar Hall
32 Archives

Central Courtyard

Back on the road, head on through **Míres**, the true agricultural centre of the Messará Plain. The Minoan **Palace of Festós**, on top of a hill, affords a marvellous view out over the Messará Plain, with its olive groves, vineyards and fields of grain, across to the Psilorítis range, and the villages dotting the opposite slopes. The layout of the palace is similar to that at Knossós, but on a much smaller scale, with the various wings grouped around a central courtyard, procession-ways and a 20-metre (22-yard) long monumental staircase. The famous *discus,* or disk, of Festós, with its hieroglyphic incriptions, is probably the most significant find.

During Minoan times, a cobbled road led to the so-called **Villa of Aghía Triátha**, 3km (1.8 miles) away, above the Libyan Sea. Here, the major finds were valuable frescoes, as well as an entire archive of clay tablets. The complex has been dated to before 1550BC, but there are still questions about its significance: it was clearly designed according to a scheme different from that of the palaces.

For the drive back to Irákleion, we recommend the scenic detour (via the turn-off for the east this side of Aghía Varvára) through the mountain village of **Aghios Thomás**. Grouped around bizarre boul-

View of the Palace of Festos

ders, only a few of the town's former 38 churches are still standing: the restored Byzantine **Aghios Thomás Church** in the market square is particularly worth seeing. If you would like a short rest before driving on, try one of the *kafeneía* on the main road. Spring visitors should try to time their visit with the annual celebration of St Thomas's day, on the first Sunday after Easter.

73

Lassíthi

In 1889, Sfakiotes from Crete's 'Wild West' founded a settlement on the Gulf of Mirabéllo, naming it after the small Byzantine church nearby, Aghios Nikólaos; today called simply 'Aghios'. Since the early 1960s, Aghios Nikólaos has been the scene of an incredible tourist boom. Although the city has neither an airport nor a large harbour and its beaches are unattractive, the centre, with its beautiful old tile-roofed houses surrounding the small harbour and the freshwater lake, has the flair of a place where one can spend one's holidays in style.

Orientation is simple, everything is easy to locate, and the northern coast has not been destroyed. The city lives off tourism and, from April to October, this factor is even more dominant than in other Cretan towns. During winter, things are quieter, and most of the countless restaurants and many of the shops close.

Although Aghios Nikólaos is a young city, the urban site itself and the surrounding countryside have a history which stretches back much further in time. In antiquity, a Dorian port was located further inland here, on the Goulá Heights. In 1206, Enrico Pescatore claimed the spot for Genoa, founding the Castello di Mirabello, the 'Fort with the Pretty View', atop the ruins of the ancient city situated on the low foothills. Henceforth, this fort lent its name to the entire region, taking on the Cretanised form of 'Merambéllo'. In 1905, Aghios Nikólaos became the capital of the Nomós Lassíthi, one of the most fertile areas of the island, containing the governmental districts of Merambéllo, Lassíthi, Ierápetra and Sitía. Once a year, on Saint Nicholas's Day, of course, Aghios Nikólaos honours its patron saint. On this occasion, local celebrities, the Bishop of Pétra, and numerous visitors gather around the Church of Aghios Nikólaos, one of the oldest and most beautiful churches on Crete.

Lassíthi Plateau

Picturesque Aghios Nikólaos

Stroll beside the sea in which the goddesses Athena and Artemis once bathed; bathing and water sports on Almyrós Beach; the Church of Aghios Nikólaos, with its painted Byzantine interior.

Aghios Nikólaos harbour

You needn't worry about finding a good meal or a place to lay your head in this resort town: there are both restaurants and hotels in abundance here, and the tourist information office at the bridge is always glad to help out with addresses, maps and tips about where to rent cars and bikes, who offers excursions by boat or bus, etc. These days, life in the city tends to focus on the small, 64-metre (210-feet) deep **freshwater Lake Voulisméni** – also called Xepato-méni, 'the bottomless one'. In 1903, the lake emitted sulphuric vapours, which nourished the theory that it is connected somehow to the Santorini volcano. The Voulisméni is surrounded by restaurants where you may not be able to enjoy the full gamut of Cretan cuisine, but you will certainly dine in lovely surroundings. According to myth, this is the lake where the goddesses Athena and Vritómartis, the Cretan Artemis, bathed.

Heading uphill on **Odós Paleóglou**, you will come to the **Ar-**

View of Aghios Nikólaos

chaeological **Museum**, situated in the section of town named after the original Arab settlers, **Arápika**. The exhibits include Minoan finds. From this elevation, you also have a beautiful view of the coast stretching northwards towards Eloúnda and Pláka; of the little island of Aghïï Pántes, a preserve of the wild goat, or *kri-krí*; and of the tiny island called Mikró Nisí, to the east of the city.

From **Kazárma**, the quarter above Lake Voulisméni, you have a clear view of Mirabéllo Bay and the city, spread out over the Kefáli Hills. Down below, the former centre of town, **Plateía E Venizélou**, can be reached via Odós Iróön Politechníou. A monument, surrounded by greenery in the middle of the square, was erected to honour the 400 people shot by the Germans to the south-west of the city in 1943. From here, Odós S Venizélou will take you down to the KTEL bus terminal, with its simple *souvláki tavérnes,* a bit removed from the hustle and bustle. Not far from here, below the road to Sitía, you will find the largest beach near the city, the **Almyrós**, with a full range of water sporting activities. Along the shoreline drive leading from the beach back to the city, the breakwater, consisting of concrete pilings spaced a metre apart, will give you an idea of how rough the sea gets here in winter. **Kitroplateiá Bay**, where the *kítra*, the citrus fruit, used to be loaded, is now used as a beach. The drive continues to the harbour, where the ships and boats pitch and toss, and where once a week a steamer drops anchor on its return voyage (via the Cycladic islands to Kárpathos and Rhodes) to its home port of Piraeus.

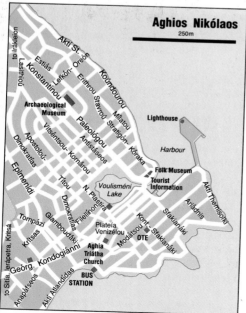

Aghios Nikólaos
250m

From the bridge across the canal, Odós 28 Oktomvríou leads to **Odós Iróön Politechníou**, which in turn ends at **Kefáli Hill**, where the Genoese erected their **Castello di Mirabéllo**. Next to the tourist information office, the white building with the brilliant blue shutters houses the **Folklore Museum**, with its interesting collection of traditional costumes, hand-woven textiles and Byzantine icons.

The city's oldest anchorage is north of the road to Eloúnda, in the small Aghios Nikólaos Cove. Not far away, on the grounds of the Minos Palace Hotel, is the church after which the city was named – built no later than the 10th century. Unfortunately, the painted interior, the only one of its kind on Crete, has been only partially preserved. Dating back to the period of controversy regarding the worship of images, and the representation of human beings in church art, the wall decoration here represents some of the rarest Byzantine painting in all of Greece. Later, the ornamental frescoes were partially painted over. You can ask for the key at the reception desk of the **Minos Palace Hotel**.

Lake Voulisméni

If you feel up to more sightseeing after this tour, we recommend a detour to the rustic town of **Neápolis**, or 'New City', 12km (7 miles) away. Laying out the broad streets and large squares here, Pasha Adosídis intended to make this town the capital of the newly-created Nomós Lassíthi. This is also the town where, several centuries earlier, in 1409, a son of poor peasants set out into the world. This native son with humble beginnings was later to become Pope Alexander V. Above Neápolis is the site of ancient Dréros, of which only a few ruins remain.

The Lassíthi Plateau

The fertile highlands between the majestic peaks of the Díkti Mountains; a monastery, and an exemplary folklore museum; the Díkti Cave. A whole day's tour.

The road winds its way up, slope by slope, through Aghios Konstantínos, Amigdáli and Zénia, and the scenery gets greener as you go. There are olive groves, fruit and plane trees and, to the left, the bare, majestic peaks of the Díkti range. In summer, the tourists set out at about 11am, so we recommend you get an early start from Aghios Nikólaos or drive up to the plateau the previous afternoon.

Once the granary of the Venetians, the **Lassíthi Plateau**, at an elevation of over 800m (2,625ft), is one of the most fertile regions on Crete due to an abundance of water derived from melting winter snows. Practically everything grows here except citrus and olive trees: grain, vegetables, fruit, lentils and chick peas. The farmers here complain bitterly about their competitors, the greenhouse-owners, who flood the market with their cheap vegetables. Since 1890, the windmills here, with their canvas sails, have served to pump up water from the limestone; and to an extent, they still do. More and more, however, the mills are being replaced by diesel pumps. However, adhering to their motto ('You never know what will happen') the Lassithiotes have played it safe and have left the old windmill frames standing, just in case

The peaks of the **Díkti Mountains** embrace the 60km² (21 square mile) plain which, from above, resembles a hand-woven carpet. It is patterned with soft, wavy lines and its 21 villages are all situated along the outer edges of the plain so as not to waste so much as a square metre of the fertile earth. These villages are inhabited by over 5,000 people, though many of the younger Lassithiotes work in the coastal tourist trade in summer. During the winter, everyone with school-age children and no land to till in the lowlands remains up here on the plateau.

They say that here, in the Greek Switzerland, the climate is so healthy that the people can do without doctors. The eight passages up onto the plateau were so narrow that

The way up to the Díkti Cave

Street trader

two people found it difficult to squeeze past each other and thus
these access routes were easy to defend. It is no wonder that this
natural fortress was at the heart of many revolts and constituted a
safe haven throughout history. Addressing the heavy resistance here,
the Venetians deemed it a 'thorn in the heart of Venice' and so prohibited all cultivation and pastoral agriculture in Lassithi for two
centuries. Violators had one leg amputated. Later, however,
Venetian engineers constructed irrigation systems which are still op-
erational today.

We begin our tour of the plateau at the **Kristallénia Monastery**,
where the *paniyíri* of the Panagheía Church is celebrated on 15 August annually, the 'name day' of the Virgin. The abbot here reaches
into a bookcase in the tiny monastery library and pulls out a 17th-
century tome as though it were a worn-out detective novel! Elsewhere, it would surely be locked up behind glass.

In **Aghios Geórgios**, the **folklore museum**, organised in an exemplary manner and housed in an old, windowless building, documents
the life of an earlier century, showing household furnishings, crafts
and agricultural implements.

The main attraction of this area is un-
doubtedly the **Díkti Cave**, situated above
Psychró, which you need not visit. This
is the cave where the Great Goddess
was worshipped from as early as 2000
BC on. Later, the Greeks established
the cave as the birthplace of the
almighty father of their gods, Zeus.
In the myth, Chronos ate all his
newborn children out of fear that
they would oust him from power.
When it came time for her to bear
Zeus, Chronos's wife Rhea out-
witted her tyrannical cannibal
of a husband, saving the infant

Harvest time

79

by giving birth in a cave. Crete's Díkti and Ida Caves both lay claims to be this mythic site, though the dispute has been settled by calling one the birthplace and the other the nursery of the god. The hike up to the entrance takes 15 minutes, and seems a lot longer in high summer, so there are 'donkey taxis' available. Below Ambelos, with its stone mills, which is one of the points of access to the plateau, there is a path from Kerá up to the **Karfí**, a peak visible

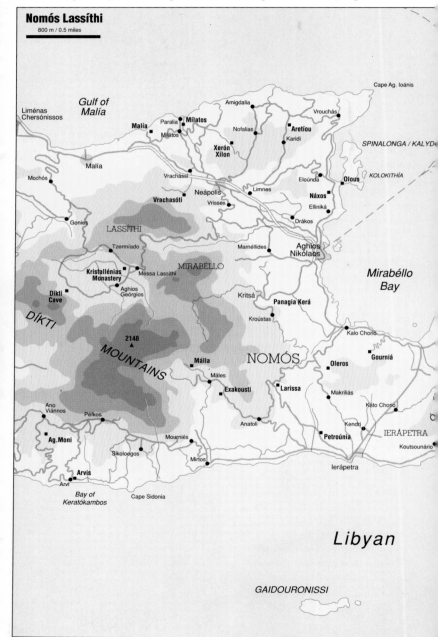

from far and wide and a Minoan shrine and sanctuary. The hike up takes about an hour and a half; you should follow the red markings and as usual try and avoid the middle of the day in high season when the sun is at its most merciless. Only the foundations of the settlement are left, but while enjoying the view from this vantage point you can imagine what those Cretan recluses of yesteryear must have felt, living up here.

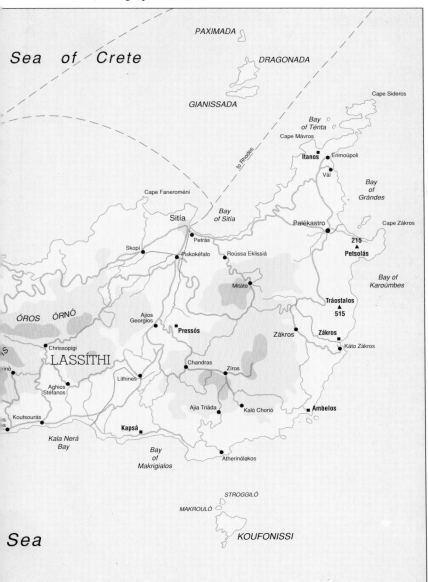

Fresh Fish and Palm Trees

A remote natural landscape; the quiet town of Sitía; authentic Cretan cuisine and delicious fish; the palm grove of Váï; the Toploú Monastery. A whole day's excursion.

The road from Aghios Nikólaos to Sitía runs high along rugged coast, lined with oleander, broom, pines and cypress trees. Here the road is as narrow as in antiquity, which is one reason why eastern Crete is still somewhat undeveloped. The drive takes you through villages and along the slopes of hills contoured with narrow terraces covered in vines.

South-west of **Chamézi**, look for the Minoan **'Oval' House** perched on a hill. The path through the fields is poorly signposted, but the hill is easy to spot. Experts are still unsure as to whether this was a sacred building or a dwelling. As is so often the case, the view is worth the detour. As base and starting point for tours of eastern Crete, **Sitía** (population: 9,000) is a sensible alternative for those seeking an alternative to crowded Aghios Nikólaos. The houses are set into the steep western coast of Sitía Bay, and the narrow little-travelled roads are connected by stairs.

Some finds from the area of the city indicate a Minoan past. Looming over Sitía, the Venetian-Turkish **Kazárma Fortress** is an impressive sight. Today it is used for theatre performances and concerts. Sitía is a stolid little provincial town with limited tourism as

Harbour and Kazárma Fortress

Palm trees in Vái

yet, and small hotels and boarding houses. In the upper part of town, you will find a small **folklore museum** worth seeing in Odós Arkadíou, and the **Archaeological Museum**, with finds from eastern Crete, on the road to Ierápetra. Down in the harbour, there is one restaurant after another facing **Plateía Venizélou**. If you are looking for something really 'authentic', try **Kalí Kardía** (the 'Good Heart'), at 20G Odós Foundalídou, a *kafeneíon/tavérna* above the harbour, with good, plain food. The **Klimatriá Tavern**, with its pretty garden, on the road to Ierápetra is also recommended. From Sitía, there are ship connections once a week to Piraeus and Rhodes via Aghios Nikólaos, as well as air connections several times weekly to Athens, Kárpathos and Rhodes.

Eastern Crete consists of mountainous hill country. Barely 800m (2,625ft) high, barren and a delicate shade of yellow, the region is reminiscent of African landscapes. The contours of the mountains are softer, gentler than in the west, the olive trees lower and bushier, and here and there the earth has an aubergine hue. The houses have flat roofs, offering the wind, which can be quite brisk at times, less resistance. To the south-east of Sitía you will come to **Palékastro**. Its offshore peninsula is the easternmost point on Crete. Two kilometres (1.2

The Minoan 'Palace' at Káto Zákros

miles) below the town, excavation work on one of the most important Minoan ports has been under way since the turn of the century. To the left of the gravel road – it cannot be paved due to the ancient remains which may still lie beneath the surface – is the fish **tavérna**, **Ee Chióna**. The view and the fish are both fabulous. Lucullus, the Roman gourmet, praised the fish from Palékastro, claiming it to be the finest anywhere.

The windy drive through the karstic landscape takes you down to **Káto Zákros**, where archaeologists have unearthed the smallest Minoan palace found to date. Above the extremely fertile land along the Zákros River where the palace lies, you will discover the mouth of the glorious Zákros Canyon – named 'Valley of the Dead' after the cave-tombs found here. The several restaurants in town and the pebble beach are reasons to spend some time here. On your way back to Sitía, you will want to see the palm grove at Váï, which is unique in Greece. Cretan palm trees only exist at five places on the island. Outlawed during the time of Pythagoras as a pagan symbol of victory, the palm was still used to decorate temples and, even today, churches. On the beach at Váï, tourism has arrived in earnest.

Twenty kilometres (12 miles) east of Sitía there is a Cretan monastery, looming up like a defensive fort amidst the barren wasteland. Consecrated to the Panagheía Akrotiriuní, **Toploú Monastery** was a place of refuge and a centre of uprisings during the Turkish occupation. During World War II, the Germans shot the abbot here when they discovered a secret radio transmitter in the monastery. The most beautiful icon in the church is that portraying the Panagheía Amólinton, the Immaculate Virgin Mary.

Toploú Monastery

Dorian Idyll

Lató Etéra, ancient Dorian city; the majestic village of Kritsá, with an especially beautiful church; the Katharó Plateau, far from madding crowd. A half day's trip.

This side of Kritsá, look for the gravel road turning off to **Lató Etéra**. This is the site of the best-preserved Cretan city dating back to the 1st millenium BC. High up, easy to defend and not visible from the sea, all the Dorian cities have enchanting views. This one owes its name to Lató, a goddess worshipped in this area. Laid out in terraces, the excavated city includes private dwellings, workshops, temples, an *agorá*, or public market-place, a city gate and stairs.

Kritsá, a majestic village 11km (7 miles) from Aghios Nikólaos, has expanded up a slope at the foot of steep cliffs. The church, surrounded by cypress trees at the entrance to the village, **Panagheía Kyrá**, consecrated to the Virgin, has three naves and supporting pillars. Its three apses and cupola date back to the 13th–14th century. In no other church are so many frescoes so well preserved as here. It is worth buying a guide book which describes the church's architecture and holdings in the shop next door, since you are not allowed to take pictures inside the church.

From Kritsá, follow the gravel road 16km (10 miles) up to the summer home of the villagers, the **Katharó Plateau** (1,100m/3,609ft). Keep your eyes open as you pass several kermes oaks and you may see goats clambering around *in* them! This road takes you to another world, far from the bustle of summer tourism, a landscape full of tranquillity and simplicity towered over by **Mt Lázaros** (2,000m/6,562ft), the tallest peak in the Díkti range. This is an ideal area for hiking.

There are several *kafeneía* where you can stop for refreshment, but it is still a good idea to pack a small picnic for this tour. Hikers will want to equip themselves with sturdy shoes, sun hats and adequate water for climbing during summer.

Lató

30 m

1 Town Gate
2 Path with Steps
3 Tower
4 Dyer's Workshop
5 Bakery
6 Public Square
7 Tomb
8 Stoa
9 Agora
10 Cistern
11 Sanctuary
12 Exedra (Gallery)
13 Towers
14 Ceremonial Steps
15 Prytaneion (Conference Room)
16 Dining Hall

Minoan Gourniá

An impressively located monastery with a breathtaking view; the fully excavated Minoan city of Gourniá; the city of Ierápetra. A half a day.
On the road to the town of Sitía, 7km (4 miles) the other side of Kaló Horió ('Good Village'), there is a turn-off to the right onto a gravel road up the mountain to the **Moní (Monastery of) Faneroménis**.

The 6-kilometre (4-mile) long stretch up the mountain is steep and full of curves. The monastery clings to the cliff like a fortress, but there is nothing here of particular interest to art historians. Still, here on this steep slope, with its breathtaking view of Mirabéllo Bay, you realise how remote most Cretan monasteries were in centuries past, when the way to the next village had to be made on foot. The church, consecrated to the Panagheía Kímissis, the Assumption of the Virgin Mary, is built into the rock. On 15 August, the day when the Dormition or Assumption of the Virgin is celebrated throughout Greece, there is a celebration here in honour of the Virgin. (Visitors should note that most Greek Marys or Marias celebrate their name day on this date.)

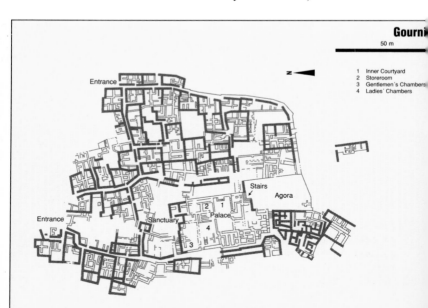

Gourniá

50 m

1 Inner Courtyard
2 Storeroom
3 Gentlemen's Chambers
4 Ladies' Chambers

Entrance

Stairs
Agora

Entrance   Sanctuary   Palace

Gourniá, the excavated Minoan city

In a broad delta, at the foot of a low, gently sloping hill directly above the sea, archaeologists discovered the ancient Minoan city of **Gourniá**. It consisted of houses crowded together along narrow alleyways. The houses had workshops and supply rooms on the ground floors, and living and sleeping quarters in the upper storeys. The only Minoan city to have been fully excavated, it had its heyday during the period of the New Palaces between 1600 and 1450 BC.

Beyond Pachiá Ammos ('Fat Sand') you join the road to Ierápetra and pass through the island's 'wasp waist', the narrowest place on Crete. Half-way there, in Episkopí, look for the 11th–12th-century **Church of Aghios Geórgios and Harálamabos** with its two naves and cupola. Descending to the sea, you reach **Ierápetra** – with its 8,600 inhabitants, the major town of the southern coast. It lies on a fertile plain, which has been disfigured by the advent of endless, plastic greenhouses. However, the structures have brought a certain affluence to the city. Ierápetra has the lowest average rainfall and the highest number of sunny days in Europe and the quay – with its queue of restaurants and cafés – is reminiscent of an Italian lakeside resort. Unfortunately, the small Venetian fort dating to 1212 is not open to the public, and all that is left of the former Turkish Quarter is a single, dilapidated mosque.

For the sake of the wonderfully scenic drive and the beautiful view, head back through the mountains via the towns of Kalamáfka, Anatolí and Máles.

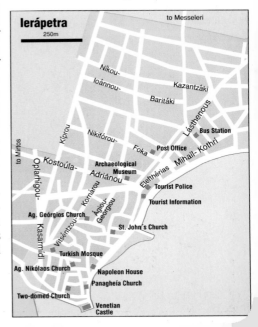

Eloúnda and Spinalónga

A popular resort; a scenic peninsula once used as a leper colony. A half day's excursion.

Eloúnda is the holiday resort frequented by so many Greek politicians. Like Aghios Nikólaos, it has undergone rapid development during recent years, due to its proximity to the trendy city and its long sandy beach. The heights around Eloúnda contain mineral deposits unique in Greece. The adjacent Spinalónga Peninsula, separated from the mainland by a canal since 1897, makes it seem as though Eloúnda lies beside an inland lake.

Below Eloúnda, where stone windmills remain standing and you can still see the former saltworks, the land was once settled but the ancient city of **Oloús** now lies below the waterline. When the sea is calm, you can still see the remains of Oloús's walls in the sea. On the opposite side, to the right above the restaurant, have a look at the fenced-in mosaic floor of an Early Christian basilica. In the summertime, boats leave hourly for Spinalónga – more properly, the islet of Kalydón, all of 80,000m^2 (95,700 square yards).

In 1579, the Venetians turned the rock into a fort. With its 35 cannons, it was considered impregnable until the Turks finally managed to conquer it. During the uprisings against the Ottomans, many Turkish families fled into the stronghold, forming their own community of 1,112 people in 1834.

Eloúnda

Kalydón/Spinalónga: the former leper colony

In 1903, the Cretan government established a leper colony on **Kalydón/Spinalónga**. Four hundred people suffering from Hansen's Disease who, until then, had been ostracised by society, now found a kind of refuge. There were workshops, restaurants and shops on the islet; church services were held in two churches; plays were performed. The healthy children of afflicted parents were taken off Spinalónga. It was not until 1957 that the colony was closed, the last in all of Greece. The residents were brought to a hospital, and the island was abandoned. As they fall into ruin, the buildings and the poignant island cemetery tell their own story of courage and a visit here is inspirational.

Bringing this outing to a close, we recommend the drive to **Pláka**, with its long pebble beach, where you can sit in one of the fish *tavérnes,* and enjoy the beautiful view of sand-coloured fortification walls and the buildings of the former colony while tucking into your fried squid or red mullet.

The old windmills north of Eloúnda

Everything grown on Crete is infinitely better than the same things grown anywhere else.

Plinius

Greek Cuisine

The common but erroneous assumption is that Greek cookery represents a deviant form of Turkish cuisine. In reality, Ottoman culinary arts benefitted from rubbing shoulders with the independent, 2,500-year-old Greek tradition – which, on Crete, is even older.

The main ingredients bubbling in Cretan as well as in Greek pots are vegetables: peas and beans (since Minoan times, both fresh and dried); artichokes; wild greens; dandelions, leeks and spinach; various types of cabbage; wild asparagus; stalk celery and onions; as well as, since Columbus's voyage to America, potatoes, tomatoes, aubergines and corn. Leafy parsley, dill, mint, garlic, spring onions and, especially, lemons are all used as well in abundance.

The main meal of the Cretan day is served at around 2pm, and consists of meat and vegetables or perhaps prawns; boiled leafy vegetables, dressed with olive oil and lemon juice; rice with spinach, or cooked black-eyed peas; fish,

steamed in the oven with lemon wedges; tomatoes, bell peppers, grape leaves or zucchini (both fruit and blossoms) stuffed with rice, ground beef and herbs – the list of possibilities is a long one. Stuffed grape and cabbage leaves, *stifádo* (spicy meat stew), cheese puffs and *maroúli* (lettuce) salad, as well as the sweets *bougátsa* and *loukoumáthes* were already known to the Ancient Greeks.

The popularity of the omnipresent 'Greek Salad', or *horiatikí saláta*, owes as much to the ease of preparation as to the seasonal

availability of its obligatory ingredients, cucumbers and tomatoes. Otherwise, there is one salad available almost all year round: *maroúli*, like 'Romaine' lettuce, finely chopped and seasoned with olive oil, dill and spring onions. Also ubiquitous are salads made of white cabbage, spinach, carrots, small and large radishes and beet-root. The various vegetables may also be cooked and served as side dishes. Pork with *maroúli* or celery stalks, for example, is exquisite.

The staple tourist dish – grilled shishkebab, or *souvláki* – is rarely eaten in Cretan homes. Most restaurants serve 'fast *tavérna* food' – meat, or sometimes fish, on the grill; baked savoury

91

puddings such as *pastítsio*, made with macaroni and minced meat; *moussaká*, made of potatoes and aubergines (often from canteen kitchens) – all of which involve less work than the tastier, vegetable-intensive dishes.

The predominant Cretan attitude is that foreigners do not enjoy most traditional fare. Restaurant cuisine *per se* did not take hold in Greece, and thus also on Crete, until the advent of tourism in the 1960s – but now there are a few genuine gourmet restaurants, and you can take your pick of Indian, Chinese, Japanese, French or German cuisines in developed areas.

At the classic Greek *estiatórion*, the up-market cousin of the *tavérna*, you will find dishes also served in Greek homes, the preparation of which is an art form: chick pea or fish soup, broad beans with artichokes, stuffed vegetables or potatoes with chicken. The simpler version of the *estiatórion* is the *mayériko*, a cooking stall where you select your food directly from the hot stove. *Miá merítha* is one portion – ie, a plateful. It is not customary to take a bit of this and a bit of that from the various pots.

In *tavérnes,* the food is freshly prepared: that is, both fish and meat are prepared over the charcoal fire, either grilled or broiled; vegetables are deep-fried or steamed; various salads, among them *melitsanosaláta*, a sort of aubergine purée, and *taramosaláta,* a purée of fish roe, are freshly made.

The classic among Cretan culinary venues is the *kafeneíon*. Here, at that bastion of the Greek male, the café, customers pass their time discussing politics, playing *távli* (Greek backgammon) and cards, reading newspapers or watching the passing parade. Here, they drink Greek coffee in small cups: *métrio,* medium sweet; *varí glikó*, strong and sweet; or *skéto*, without sugar. In recent years, instant coffee has become very popular – with 'Nescafé' standing in for all brands – hot with milk or cold in the form of a *frappé* with an ample head of foam. In the village *kafeneíon*, not off limits to women, the proprietor will also crack an egg into a skillet, make a salad or open a tin for hungry guests.

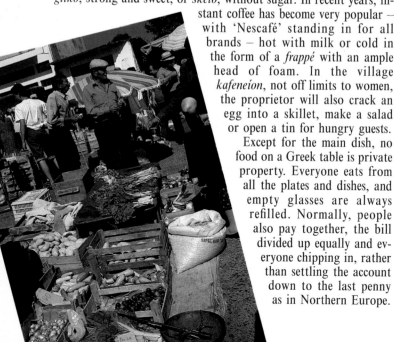

Except for the main dish, no food on a Greek table is private property. Everyone eats from all the plates and dishes, and empty glasses are always refilled. Normally, people also pay together, the bill divided up equally and everyone chipping in, rather than settling the account down to the last penny as in Northern Europe.

Cretan Venues

Tsigoutháthika or *rakáthika* are typical Cretan drinking venues where the traditional tipple of the island, the homemade white liquor, *tsigouthiá*, or *rakí*, is served, accompanied by various appetisers, *mezéthes*, which are quite filling. (One truly Cretan speciality is *oftés patátes*, potatoes roasted in their skins.) In an *ouzerí*, on the other hand, *oúzo* is the main drink. On many street corners you will find *souvlatzíthika*, where you eat chunks of grilled meat with bites of tomato, onions and *tzatzíki* (yoghurt, cucumber, garlic and dill) – all wrapped up in pitta bread – either on the spot or as a

takeaway. One note: when selecting a place to dine, keep in mind that a *tavérna* is the Greek equivalent of the French bistro, while an *estiatórion* is a classier, more expensive restaurant.

Desserts

The *zakaroplasteíon* specialises in all kinds of sweets: from ice-cream to *rizógalo* (rice pudding), puddings, pies, cake-like pastries, such as *bougátsa, loukoumáthes* and *pástes*. Fresh oranges and mandarines for dessert have only been popular since around 1500, and coffee, which today seems so essential to the Greek way of life, arrived in Greece and Crete from Ethiopia in around 1600.

Celebrations and Nightlife

The *kritiká kéntra,* traditional nightclubs located on the edges of towns or even further out in the country, are important addresses for weddings, or evenings of live Cretan music. People also come here to eat and drink, but mainly to dance Cretan dances. The

'Wedding rings'

skiláthika are similar but sleazier clubs – actually imports from the mainland – their dance music furnished by second- or third-rate *bouzoúki* ensembles. Whisky is sold by the bottle for steep prices. A *skiláthiko* is the final stop of many a late-evening tour of the nightspots. In addition, there are plenty of bars and discos which do not fill up until the wee hours, and countless café-bars where you can order anything from coffee to whisky.

The restaurants, cafés and bars listed below are predominately patronised by locals and are not always easy to find, so you will need a taxi. These places will give you a good idea of everyday cooking and dining out on Crete. So: *Kalí órexi* – enjoy your meal!

Dining in Chaniá

AERIKO, *taverna/ouzerí;* Aktí Miaoúli in the quarter of Kum Kapí.

TAMAM, *estiatórion*; in a former Turkish bath at Odós Zambelíou 49, on the harbour.

GONIA, a tiny restaurant with western Cretan specialities such as *sfakianés pítes* and *kalitsoúnia*, cheese puffs from Sfakiá and Chaniá. Opens at 6pm. Odós Polichronídi 33/corner of Odós Geróla in the quarter of Páno Kum Kapí.

LES VAGABONDS, French cuisine; Odós Pórtou 44.

BINGASA, *estiatórion*. To the west of town in Galatás on the main road. Turkish and Greek food.

KULURIDIS, *tavérna* in Vamvakópoulo. Follow the signs south-west along the road to Alikianós. Very good cuisine, but not cheap.

MALAXA, small *tavérna* in the village of the same name to the east of town. Speciality: *stáka,* flour cooked in cream, eaten with bread.

KIANI AKTI, classical fish *tavérna* under tamarisks directly by the sea on the road to the east just this side of Kalíves (closed in winter).

TSIKUDADIK, on the main road in Soúda, opposite the mill; lovely appetisers (*mezéthes*).

MELTEMAKIA, fish *tavérna* on the road from Soúda in the direction of the airport, in Wlités at the end of the bay (closed from December through to February).

BARBAS LEFTÉRIS, *tavérna* in Kamissianá, just this side of Kolimbári towards the west of town.

PAPAGALLOS, bar, Odós Kondiláki near the harbour.

FAGOTTO, bar, Odós Angélon 16. In an old vaulted building near the Firkás Fortress.

MELTÉMI, *kafeneíon* next to the Marine Museum.

CLUB KANALI, disco, Aktí Tombási.

STREET, disco bar, on the old harbour.

Dining in Réthymnon

AVLI, restaurant; Odós Xanthoudídou, corner of Odós Radamánthios. Very refined, with candlelight and piano music.

SOKRATIS, *estiatórion* at the Rimondi Fountain (closed in winter).

SÉRIFOS, fish *tavérna* on the Venetian harbour.

KIRIA MARIA, *mayériko* on Odós Moschowíti near the Rimondi Fountain.

SOKAKI, *tavérna/estiatórion*; Odós Pórtou 6 (closed in the winter).

BALUARDO, *mezethopolíon* (equivalent to a *tsigoutháthiko*); on the seaside drive below the Fortézza near the harbour.

TO METHISMENO FEGGARI, ('The Drunken Moon'), *ouzerí/kafeneíon*, Odós Melisínou 34.

JEORJIOS, *rakáthiko*, below the Archaeological Museum (closed in the winter).

MONA, *rakáthiko*; Odós Ag. Barbáras 13. Here they serve only *oftés patátes,* green olives and *tsigouthiá/rakí.*

KOMBOS, *tavérna* in Violí Haráki on the old road to Chaniá

MILTOS, in Maroulás, to the west of town. *Tavérna* serving two hot dishes a day, such as lentils or aubergines.

O PSARAS, simple, typical fish *tavérna*. Odós Arambatsóglu 69 (formerly Odós Thessaloníkis). You should try the *stifádo* with *ochtapódi* (octopus in red sauce) here.

SESILIA, bar, Prokiméa E Venizélou.

GALERO, café-bar at the Rimondi Fountain.

FORTETZA, disco on the Venetian harbour.

Dining in Irákleion

Kossos, *estiatórion*; opposite the Morosini Fountain. A respectable eating place serving good plain food.

3/4, restaurant, bar, café; Odós Theotokopoúlou 1. In a pretty, neoclassical building on the old harbour; very refined.

Doré, café and restaurant with roof garden on the fifth floor, Plateía Eleftherías. For elegant dining out.

Giovanni, *tavérna*, Odós Koraí.

Ippokambos ('Sea Horse'), *ouzerí;* Odós Mitsotáki 3, on the old harbour (closed from 3.30–7pm).

Vardia, ('Shift'), *ouzerí* on the old harbour, opens at 4pm.

Konstandin Lidakis, café-bar in Arhánes, opposite the Panagheía Church with its three naves on the main road.

Bugatsa, tiny shop at the Morosoni Fountain; puff pastry with a cream cheese or sweet cream filling – also to take out.

Irida, café, Odós Koraí 1. In a marvellous neoclassical building.

Onar, café and tearoom; Odos Chandakos 36B.

Tromboni, 'boite', Odós S Venizélou, corner of Melidóni.

Avantage, cafeteria; Odós Chándakos 12.

Flu, Plateía Daskalogiánni. (*Flou* means 'out of focus'.)

Flash, Bistro and **Avgo**, bars at the end of Odós Koraí.

Dining in Aghios Nikólaos

Tavern Aquas, *tavérna* with tables, Odós Paleológou, 100m (110yds) from the Folklore Museum. Also numerous hot dishes.

Tavern the Pine, traditional *estiatórion* by the lake.

Itanos, old-style *estiatórion* on Odós D'yprou.

La Casa, *tavérna*, Odós 28 Oktombríou, with lake view.

Aktéon, simple *tavérna* on the harbour.

O Sigos, *estiatórion* in Kaló Horió on the road to Sitía.

O Vioz einai oneiron, *mezethopolíon/ tavérna*, Odós Pasifáis 1.

Fish Tavérnes in Plaka

Fifteen kilometres (9 miles) to the north with a view of Spinalónga Island.

The Café, Odós Nik Plastíra 26, above the lake with a beautiful view; small portions.

Café Plaza, next to the Folklore Museum. A bit chic and expensive, but right in the heart of things.

Bora-Bora, Lipstick, Studio Disco Video and **Disco Yachting Club** are all discos on the harbour.

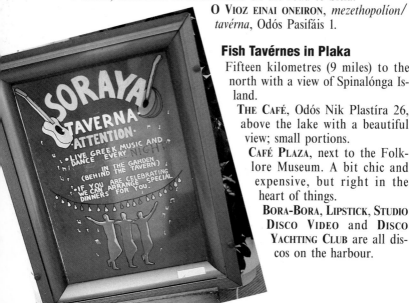

Shopping

Ceramics, embroidery work, hand woven fabrics, knits and metal and wood crafts, as well as spices and herbal teas – such as mint, sage and *diktamo* – are all popular

souvenirs that have been important export commodities on Crete as far back as Minoan times. The shops are concentrated in the town centre areas of Chaniá, Réthymnon, Irákleion and Aghios Nikólaos. The souvenirs-only shops, selling plenty of kitsch and junk, are naturally easy to recognise – and avoid. The merchandise sold here usually has little to do with folk art or culture.

Spices: In Chaniá, for example, the covered market is truly a paradise for spice fans: from curry to red peppercorns to Cretan saffron in three different strengths, you can find everything here. Choose from spicy cinnamon bark, boiled to make tea in the winter, along with the most important spice in Greek cooking, next to the lemon, *rígani*, or wild marjoram.

Household Goods: Small household goods shops and market vendors sell sturdy, woven wicker baskets, as well as light airy ones out of bamboo, wonderful wooden spoons and the traditional *bríki* – the small copper coffee pot with the long handle. With a bit of luck, you can also find the matching long-handled copper spoon and the whisk, the Greek coffee implements which have been out of fashion for quite some time. You may have to look for a chinaware store to get the tiny cups to go with the set: the classical *kafeneíon* variety are white and unbreakable. To round out your coffee utensils you also need a brass coffee grinder. The smaller versions of these mills double quite well as peppergrinders.

Cretan Knives: Long and curved, in silver scabbards and with thick white handles, these weapons were originally part of the traditional costume. The old ones are rare and expensive, but they also come in various shapes and sizes as souvenirs. However, there is also a whole range of other knives, from chopping knives to the curved knives used to prune the grape vines (or *ambélia*).

Fabrics: Hand woven top-quality fabrics and blankets, usually on a red background, are still, like hand-embroidered or crocheted blankets, important products of the native crafts industry, although industrial copies are stepping up competition. Inexpensive items are sheep's wool knits and countless cotton products from T-shirts to towels, as well as conventional linens with colourful or monochrome stripes on a white background. These get softer with every washing.

Leathergoods: Crete, and above all Chaniá, is famous for its leathergoods: bags in all sizes, rucksacks, sandals and especially boots of cowhide imported from Africa.

Ceramics/Earthenware: Unglazed storage jars of the kind produced on Crete 4,000 years ago and usually used as flower pots today plus other pots and jugs of all sizes are often sold along the roads just outside towns. There is also a great deal of everyday earthenware, some of it quite pretty.

Jewellery: Gold and silver are relatively inexpensive in Greece, which explains the abundance of jewellery shops – often selling machine-made merchandise. Still, there are a number of skilled gold- and silversmiths.

Printed Matter: If you are interested in additional information about Crete, you can pick up literature and maps of the island at the international bookshops, as well as at many of the centrally-located kiosks.

Music: We recommend you sample some of the records or cassettes by the best known and loved Cretan musicians, such as Psarantónis and his band from Anóghia, who do interpretations – often quite unconventional ones, at that – of traditional, folk music. His *Erotókritos*, Crete's 'national' 17th-century epic, is wonderful. For something completely different, on a soft lyrical note, try the love songs and laments (*erotiká* and *mirolóya*), which Ludovíkos and Anóghia collected among the women of their village. The recordings by Ross Daly, as well, an Irishman who has practically become a Cretan, are especially creative, his *Lavírinthos,* for example. This is also true of the albums by the famous and beloved singer who died at an early age, Níkos Xilúris, Psarantónis's brother. The music by a *lyra* player who 'emigrated' to Pyraeus, Kóstas Mountákis, is to be highly recommended as well.

Culinary Products: Returning to the pleasant subject of food and drink, there are a number of products worth taking back home with you, including the sharp, firm cheese, *graviéra;* honey (*méli*), especially the kind derived from thyme blossoms; wine from the Kastélli Kissamós to Sitía; and *tsigouthiá,* Crete's version of *oúzo*. You can also stock up on *pássa témpo* from any of the numerous street carts, paper bags full of peanuts in salted shells, pistachios, roasted chick peas and pumpkin seeds, all for the journey home.

Shopping in Chaniá

The **covered market** on Plateía S
Venizélou offers a wide selection of
all Crete's various herbs, spices,
cheeses and honeys. Odós Skrídlof,
the extension of Odós Tsouderón
below the market, leading to Odós
Chálidon, is the street of the *sti-
vanáthika,* the **bootmakers-cum-
leathergoods-retailers**, where
you can also buy bags and sandals, rucksacks and belts. In
summer, the street is so
crowded that you can hardly
get through. The surrounding lanes are the place to
watch one of these boot-
makers at work. The

Street in Réthymnon

leather products are good, durable and reasonably priced.

In the former Turkish baths, the *hamám* on Odós Chálidon, a coppersmith has set up his workshop. His prettiest products: candlesticks in various sizes and narrow, cylindrical coffee grinders. For everyday pottery, try the **Trochós' Ceramics Workshop** next to the Archaeological Museum on the same street for ashtrays, vases and cups. The international **bookshop**, hidden behind all the postcard stands, stocks a wide range of foreign-language books on Crete. Not far from Aktí Tombási, the 'Artisan's Cooperative of Chaniá' runs a show- and sales-room with exhibits of hand woven table-cloths, blankets and carpets, as well as ceramics.

If healthy 'alternatives' appeal to you, then you will like the small **Stáchi** ('Ear of Grain') **Health Food Store**, on Odós Kriári just off Plateía 1866. There are also health food corners now in many of the supermarkets.

A special tip for all those with a penchant for the genuine article: locate the **General Store (spirits)** at Odós Grigoríou 16 (one block up from the city hall, *dimarhío*), for here you can still buy wine (*krassí*), brandy (*konyák*) and *tsigouthiá*, all right out of the barrel.

And, finally, below the covered market on Odós Potié, there is a small shop specialising in *távli*, the Greek version of backgammon, as well as chess sets.

Shopping in Réthymnon

The main shopping streets in Réthymnon are: Odós Arkadíou, Odós Iróön Politechníou, Odós Paleológou and Odós Gerkári. Here, too, you'll find Crete's **culinary delights** galore: honey and herbs, pickled or black and green olives in brine, spices and cheese – plus the richly ornamented 'wedding rings', used more as a decoration today than actually eaten. On Odós Paleológou, diagonally opposite the Venetian loggia, there is an **off-license** which even sells self-bottled *tsigouthiá* or *rakí*. You should at least have a look at the **Faskómilo** (sage) **Herb Shop** on Odós Soulíou, a truly original, witty store where each little packet of herbs is labelled with often rather unconventional suggestions regarding its use. The tiny leaves and branches of the *sarantothéndri* (the 'forty tree'), are good for ailments of the duodenum, the gall bladder and the liver; and, as a seasoning for shishkebab and pizza, the house recommends thyme '…without wood, without dirt, without dust…'

The international **bookshop** at the corner of Odós I Peticháki and Prokiméa E Venizélou stocks a good selection, including translations of Greek literature, art and nature guide books about Crete and excursions from Crete, as well as prints of old views of the city and maps of the island. Réthymnon also has a **health food store**: **Natúra** on Odós Kountourióti 70, not far from the city hall.

Shopping in Irákleion

Odós 1866 is to Irákleion what the covered market is to Chaniá: a colourful, bustling bazaar with countless stands selling all the culinary delights Crete has to offer. Also hidden in this street you have one of those simple old Greek hotels with rooms containing up to four beds. One of the small sidestreets features one hot food stall and *tavérna* after another. After a night of drinking, people come here at dawn to eat *patsás*, a soup made of tripe, purportedly to clear their heads. The major shopping streets are Odós Kalokerinóu, leading to the Pórta Chanión in the west, Odós 25 Avgoústou, Odós Dikeosínis, Odós Dedálou and its parallel street, Odós Koraï.

Irákleion is full of antique shops – although not everything which is sold as such is actually antique, and buyers must beware of paying top money for copies. But a pretty copy can also be very pleasing if purchased at a good price. You will find many books on Irákleion and Crete at the international **bookshop** on Odós 25 Avgoústou. The most beautiful bookshop on the island, however, is on Odós Koraï – one of the prettiest little streets in town, with numerous renovated neoclassical buildings. Browsing among the array of vol-

umes at No 4 will probably make you wish you could read Greek, but you may at least buy a print of one of the old Merian engravings of Irákleion or one of the old maps. A few houses down, at No 10, the **'Alói'** (aloe), a **health food store,** has established itself.

Opposite the Archaeological Museum on Plateía Eleftherías, Eléni Kastrinoyánni has her beautiful, large shop well known for its **hand-woven fabrics**, none inexpensive. If it is exquisite jewellery you have in mind, some of it patterned upon Byzantine prototypes, you will find it at **Fanourákis** on Plateía Fokás. Fanourakis, a Cretan jeweller, has shops in Athens as well, and his designs are especially well liked by Athenians who find Zolotas and Lalaounis too 'mass produced' and ubiquitous these days.

Shopping in Aghios Nikólaos

In this youngest and smallest of the island's urban centres, shopping is limited to the two streets beginning at the harbour, Odós Koundoúrou and Odós 28 Oktomvríou. Here, too, you have the ubiquitous jewellery and leathergoods shops; in fact, there are even some shops here where prices are listed in foreign currencies.

One shop with a tradition is the **arts and crafts shop** on Odós 28 Oktomvríou. Many years ago, owner Sofía Kaná swapped her career as a journalist for weaving. She herself collects all the plants from which she makes the dyes for her **carpets**. Many women have since learned the old dyeing methods from her. Also worth mention is a little shop a bit further up on the same side of the street, which sells cotton, woolen and wool/silk knitwear at reasonable prices. Like many others, this shop is closed from November to April – in which case you can go do your shopping at the **knitting factory**, *to plektírio*, on Odós Ethnikís Antístasis.

Saints' Days

The *paniyíria* are among the most important dates on the Cretan calendar of celebrations. These festive events honouring the patron saints of monasteries always begin the day before. In the old days, people converged on the monastery, either on foot, or by mule or donkey, bags and baskets packed with blankets for the night, wicker bottles of wine and bulging parcels of food. The car has changed the character of these feast days: today, people seldom stay overnight.

The 'name days' of the churches' saints are equally important and particularly beautiful at small, remote churches. For many, this is the one time of the year when they are blessed with any visitors. This is also one reason why there is at least a gravel road leading to even the most remote and tiny church. In the churches, priests pass out *ártos*, consecrated, sweet, white bread, sometimes followed by wine, salted fish and ordinary bread. Since there are many monasteries and countless churches, all of them having their own saints (some even two), there are an endless number of saints' days celebrated throughout Crete.

Here, then, is a selection of these religious celebrations, along with the other Cretan festive and memorial days:

1st Sunday after Easter: *Aghios Thomás* at the Vrondíssi Monastery/Irákleion.

23 April: *Aghios Geórgios* in many villages, if Easter is late – otherwise on Easter Monday.

8 May: *O Ioánnis o Theológos* (John the Evangelist) at the Preveli Monastery/Réthymnon.

20–27 May: *Ee Máchi tis Krítis* (The Battle of Crete), commemoration of the German air attack in 1941.

25 May: Celebrations in Hóra Sfakión commemorating the beginning of the 1821 Revolution.

24 June: *Ioánnis o Próthromos* (John the Baptist) and midsummer celebrations.

20 July: *Profítis Ilías* (Prophet Elijah), on mountain peaks and in many villages.

103

26 July: *Aghios Paraskeví*, popular celebration at the Skotinó Grotto in Nomós Irákleion, district of Pediáda.
July: Wine festival in Réthymnon.
6 August: *Metamórfosis*, the Transfiguration of Christ, on Mt Yoúchtas near Arhánes.
15 August: *Ee Kímissis tis Panagheías*, Assumption of the Virgin Mary, at the monasteries of Chrissoskalítissa, Faneroménis etc.
25 August: *Aghios Títos* in Irákleion.
27 August: *Aghios Fanúorios* at the former Valsamónero Monastery.
14 September: *Tímios Stavrós,* the Raising of the Cross in Axós and Anóghia, Réthymnon; procession to Aféndis Stavroménos.
3 November: *Aghios Geórgios o Methistís,* Saint George, who 'makes the others drunk' – this is the day when the new wine and the fresh *tsigouthiá* are tasted.
7–9 November: Cretan 'national' holiday at the Arkádi Monastery.
11 November: *Aghios Minás*, patron saint of Irákleion.
21 November: *Panagheías Isodia,* Mary's introduction to the Temple, the patron saint of Chanía and Réthymnon.
3 December: *Aghios Nikólaos*, patron saint of the city.

What to Know? Practical Information

When to Visit

Crete is always enjoyable, even if there are some low-hanging clouds in November, or a little thunder, or even several hours of that rain so anxiously awaited by the olive-growers. Visitors interested only in lying on the beach will choose to come in midsummer, despite the overcrowding and the heat. But, for getting to know the island well, the spring and autumn are much better seasons, with ideal weather for hikes and outings. Winter, in fact, is the perfect time to come if your particular interest is studying the Palace of Knossós and the Archaeological Museum in Irákleion, with its numerous Minoan holdings, unhurried and unhampered by the masses of other visitors. Along the coast, temperatures never fall below freezing, whereas the mountains may be covered in snow until spring.

Visa Requirements

For a stay of up to three months, travellers from Great Britain, the United States or Canada do not need a visa; a passport or identification card is required. Anyone intending to stay for a longer period must apply for a residence permit.

Air Connections

Most visitors to Crete arrive by air these days, on direct charter or regularly scheduled flights. From November to March, however, you must change planes in Athens. Airports of arrival are Chaniá and Irákleion – and still, occasionally, Sitía.

Sea Connections

The classic way to reach the island is by sea. The ferries, all belonging to Cretan shipping lines (ANEK, Minoan Lines and Rethimniakí Lines), ply the waters between Chaniá's port, Soúda, Irákleion and Réthymnon and Piraeus daily. The ships are large and comfortable, the food is inexpensive and there are cabins available, for the crossings usually take place at night. Choose this leisurely transition – instead of plunging into a totally new environment 'out of the blue'. During the summer months, there are frequent ship connections with Santoríni; once a week (all year around) a ship sails from Piraeus via the Cycladic Islands, and from Crete to Rhodes and back; as well as from Kastélli/Kíssamos via

Kythira to the Peloponnese. For yachts, the ports of call are Chaniá and Irákleion.

Tourist Information

We recommend you stop in at one of the EOT (Greek Tourist Organisation) information offices or enquire with the local authorities (Tourist Police) – where information and hotel lists are available.

Chaniá: Phantheon Building, Odós Kriári 40. Tel 0821 26426. Aktí Tombási 6. Tel 0821 43300 (during the tourist season).

Réthymnon: Prokiméa E Venizélou. Tel 0831 29148.

Irákleion: Odós Xanthoudídou 1, across from the Archaeological Museum. Tel 081 288203, 288225.

Aghios Nikólaos: Akti I Koundoúrou 20 (at the bridge). Tel 0841 22357.

Money Matters

You may change money at airports and frontier crossings, in hotels, bureaux de change and banks, but the post offices offer the best rates.

The Greek currency is the drachma. There are notes of from 50 to 5,000 drachmas and coins from one to 50 drachmas. It is prohibited to export more than 300 drachmas, but you can import any amount of foreign currency.

You should report amounts over £250/$500US upon entering if you think you may want to take this money back out of the country when you leave. Strikes permitting, banks are open Monday–Friday, 8.30am–2pm.

Accommodation

We recommend you stop in at one of the EOT (Greek Tourist Organisation) information offices or enquire with the local Tourist Police, where information and hotel lists are available.

Chaniá

AMFORA HOTEL
Category A. Tel 0821 42998.
DOMA HOTEL
Category B. Tel 0821 21772.
XENIA HOTEL
Category B. Tel 0821 24561.
PLAZA HOTEL
Category C. Tel 0821 22998.
THEOFILES HOTEL
Category C. Tel 0821 53294.

Réthymnon:

RITHIMNA BEACH HOTEL
Category A. Tel 0831 29491.
ADELE BEACH BUNGALOWS
Category B. Tel 0831 71047.
SKALETA BEACH
Category B. Tel 0831 93244.
ARMONIA HOTEL
Category C. Tel 0831 23905.
LEFTERIS HOTEL
Category C. Tel 0831 23803.

Irákleion:

XENIA HOTEL
Category A. Tel 081 284000.
KASTRO HOTEL
Category B. Tel 081 285020.
KRIS HOTEL
Category B. Tel 081 223211.
MARIN HOTEL
Category C. Tel 081 220737.

Aghios Nikólaos:

MINOS PALACE

Category Deluxe. Tel 0842 23801.
ARCHONTIKON HOTEL
Category A.
CORAL HOTEL
Category B. Tel 0842 28363.
MARIGO HOTEL
Category B. Tel 0842 28439.
DELTA HOTEL
Category C. Tel 0842 28991.

Electricity
In Greece, the household current is 220 Volts. You can get adaptors for the various electrical sockets at any supermarket.

Clothing
In summer, you should bring light clothing made of natural fabrics; in addition, we would recommend a windbreaker, jersey and sturdy shoes for evenings on board ship, at the seaside or on hikes. From December to March, you do not need a heavy coat, but you should pack ample pullovers and a rain coat, since it is often damp and both apartments and public places are often poorly heated. Sometimes, it is warmer outside than inside.

ABOUT THE ISLAND

Geography and Topography
Crete is 260km (162 miles) long, 12–60km (7–37 miles) wide, and the coastline is 1,046km (650 miles) in length. It is the largest of the Greek islands and the fifth largest in the Mediterranean. The most characteristic feature of the landscape is the silvery olive trees, whose cultivation was intensified during the rule of the Turks.

The geography of Crete is largely determined by three high massifs: the Léfka Ori (White Mountains) to the west with its highest peak, the Páchnes (2,452m/8,045ft); the Ida range, or Psiloritís (2,456m/8,058ft) in the centre; and the Díkti Mountains in the east (2,148 m/7,047ft). The mountains

in the east are gentler, with the highest peak, the Aféndis Stavroménos, reaching 1,476m/4,843ft. Crete owes its over 3,000 caves – approximately half of all the caves in Greece – and the numerous ravines to the crystalline consistency of its limestone crust. The majority of the underground cavities have yet to be explored. The gorges are predominantly located on the

southern half of the island, the longest and most famous being the Samariá Gorge. There are two large and several smaller fertile plateaux, as well as two large bays along the northern coast.

The census of 1981 counted a population of 520,000, more than half of whom live in the Nomós Irákleion. Crete is divided up into four *nomí*, governmental regions: Chaniá, Réthymnon and Irákleion, with their respective regional capitals of the same names; and Lassíthi, with Aghios Nikólaos as its capital. The individual *nomí* are subdivided into districts, or *eparchíes*. In 1972, Irákleion replaced Chaniá as the capital of the entire island. On Crete there are 11 cities and 1,447 villages.

Weather
Hippocrates, the great doctor of antiquity, recommended that anyone convalescing from a severe illness should seek out the mild climate of Crete. With an average of 320 sunny days per year, the average temperature in

the summer is 30–35°C (86–95F), rarely rising as high as 40°C (104F); in the winter it is 10–18°C (50–65F); and while the water never gets over 25°C (77F) in the summer, it is 15-21°C (60–70F) during the winter months. The hottest month is July, when conditions can become African in the truest sense of the word when, in addition to the the hot sun, the scorching desert wind, the *livas,* blows from the south. But from whatever direction the winds blow, they are a decisive factor. When the wind speed rises above eight on the Beaufort Scale, which happens quite often, nothing leaves port, not even the largest ferries. During the period from the end of May through August, a northerly trade wind prevails, the *meltémi,* blowing for about 15 days at a time. The Turkish Cretans have coined poetic epithets, such as 'grape *meltémi',* for this wind . During the summer months, you should take the sun seriously, avoiding going out during the hottest hours at midday.

Flora and Fauna

The vast wooded areas of prehistoric Crete are no more: deforestation and grazing have left but two per cent of the land area covered with trees. These are mainly cypresses, pines, oaks, chestnuts, planes, pines, tamarisks, juniper and eucalyptus trees. There are over 2,000 botanical species on Crete, of which a tenth are indigenous – numerous herbs, for example – the finest being the *díkatamos,* a wonder drug good for all sorts of illnesses and very tasty.

In addition to the native wild goat, the *krí-krí* – today a protected species – there are hares, rabbits, martens, small eagles, hawks, buzzards, lamb vultures and numerous butterflies on Crete. There are no poisonous snakes on the island. The camel's stint as a pack animal here ended with the Turkish withdrawal from the island, and the job was left to the mules and donkeys. As throughout the rest of the Mediterranean, the fish population in Crete's seas has gone down sharply.

Agriculture

Despite the growth of tourism, Crete still has an agricultural economy, although only about 35 per cent of the land can be cultivated. The most important crops are olive oil, olives, sultanas, table grapes, tomatoes, cucumbers, citrus fruits, wine, bananas and carob. Crete's flocks of sheep and goats do produce some meat but primarily wool and various types of cheese.

Earthquakes

The major portion of Crete belongs to Greece's earthquake-prone southern arc. The island lies on the Aegean Fault, which is no deeper than 500–800m (1,640–2,625ft), and there is a rift running through the southern part of the island, reaching a depth of 5,000m (3.10 miles). The last earthquake was in 1959.

GETTING AROUND

Taxis

Taxis and radio taxis are affordable and readily available; they can also be flagged down on the street. By taking taxis you benefit from the driver's knowledge of the area.

Buses

The municipal and rural bus systems (KTEL) are reliable, punctual and inexpensive. Each city has its own bus terminal (marked on the city maps) – just ask for the 'KTEL'. Timetables (also in English) can be obtained there, as well as in travel agencies and tourist information bureaux.

Car and Motorcycle Rentals

The number of car and motorcycle rental shops are legion; in fact, of late, you can even rent bicycles. We recommend you first look over both the vehicle and the insurance conditions very carefully. Many of the travel agencies also rent vehicles.

Petrol Stations

Petrol stations are open on weekdays from 7am–7pm; Saturday until 3pm. Certain petrol stations are also open all night and on Sunday. Unleaded petrol is available on Soúda Avenue just before Chaniá (Shell), 3km (1.9 miles) from Réthymnon on the road to Agía Galíni (BP) and on the road to Irákleion (Shell); in Irákleion: on Ikárou Avenue (Mobil) and in the Alikarnassós district (Eko), on the road from Irákleion just before Aghios Nikólaos (Texaco) and on the road from Aghios Nikólaos to Ierápetra (Eko).

Road Safety

There is a good network of roads, and what your road map may still show as a gravel road, may be already paved. A word of caution, nevertheless, the Cretan style of driving, being more on the defensive side, takes some getting used to. High speeds – usually not possible anyway – are not recommended, if you want to avoid hair-raising surprises, whether it be that unexpected vehicle pulling into the road, a huge pothole or rock, or an

entire herd of sheep suddenly looming up around the bend. Although usually ignored, the use of seatbelts in cars is required by law, as are helmets for motorcyclists. The maximum speeds permitted on the national highway are: 100km/h (62mph) for cars, 70 km/h (43mph) for other vehicles; the speed limit on country roads is 70km/h (43mph) and within towns usually 50km/h (31mph).

Maps and Guide Books

There is a large supply of street and road maps and guide books on the market with information about cities, museums, excavation sites, flora and fauna. So if you are a fact fiend, you can obtain a small library of material simply by stopping off at the nearest central kiosk, or *períptero*, or any of the foreign-language bookshops. The street and road maps are not always entirely accurate, by the way.

Hiking

The few services to hikers on Crete are provided through the Greek Alpinists' Club. The number of viable trails is dwindling, as more and more of the old footpaths are turned into graded roads. However, in collaboration with the Alpinists' Club, the few tour promoters offering hiking holidays have started to mark some of the trails with coloured dots.

Excursions

Recommended gear: a pocket torch (flashlight), sturdy shoes and, even in

summer, a jacket or sweater. For remote areas, an air pump is a good idea. A thermos jug of water and an early start are absolute musts in summer. From around 2–6pm is siesta time everywhere, including any of the monasteries you may want to visit. In the villages, the *kafeneíon* is the local 'information office' for overnight accommodation, and the place to get the key to the nearby church.

HEALTH & EMERGENCIES

The symbol used by Greek chemists is a red cross on a white ground. The range of non-prescription drugs is wider than in Great Britain. Business hours are equivalent to those of other shops, with Saturday, Sunday and all-

night services posted outside. There are hospitals and physicians in all the larger towns.

Hospitals:

Chaniá	(0821) 27231
Réthymnon	(0831) 27491
Irákleion	(081) 231931
Aghios Nikólaos	(0841) 22369

Police:

Chaniá	(0821) 24647
Réthymnon	(0831) 28156
Irákleion	(081) 233190
Aghios Nikólaos	(0841) 22251

HOLIDAYS & BUSINESS HOURS

On Greek Orthodox Crete, the movable dates of church holidays (such as the Monday preceding Ash Wednesday, Easter and Whitsun) are determined according to the Julian Calendar and thus seldom coincide with the equivalent holidays of the Roman Catholic and Protestant Churches. The holiest day is Easter, *Pascha*, the culmination of the 40-day fasting period (Lent), and the entire Orthodox year. The Resurrection of Christ is celebrated at midnight by the Orthodox faithful in churches throughout the island.

1 January: New Year's Day
6 January: *Ta Aghia Theofánia*, the blessing of all waters in commemoration of the Baptism of Christ.
Kathará Deftéra: Clean Monday, the Monday preceding Ash Wednesday and the beginning of the fasting period.
25 March: National holiday celebrating the beginning of the struggle against the Turks in 1821.
Megáli Paraskeví: Good Friday, the symbolic Burial of Christ with processions through villages and towns.
Páscha: Easter Sunday and Monday.
1 May: 'Labour Day' and popular outing day when the people pick flowers and bind them into wreaths to dec-

orate their cars and homes.

Pentecostí: Whit Sunday.

Aghiou Pnévmatos: Whit Monday.

15 August: *Ee Kímissi tis Panagheías*, Assumption of the Virgin Mary, one of the most important holidays.

28 October: National holiday; the Day of *Ohi*, 'no', the Greek government's answer to Mussolini's 1940 ultimatum.

25–26 December: *Christoúyenna*, Christmas.

Shops

All shops are open from 8am–1.30pm, and closed on Wednesday and Saturday afternoons, as well as all day Sunday. On the other afternoons, the grocers' shops and all the other shops are open on alternate days from 5–8:30pm. Souvenir shops and supermarkets stay open all day until late in the evening. In the villages, the *kafeneíon* often doubles as the grocery store.

Museums and Excavation Sites

The hours at sites and museums change frequently. Most sites are open in the morning until 2 or 3pm, though closed one weekday. Ask at the local tourist information office for current opening hours.

COMMUNICATION & MEDIA

Language

If you take the trouble to learn some Greek prior to embarking on your visit, you will be rewarded with praise and will make friends more easily. It is a great help to learn the Greek alphabet, even if the majority of street signs are also written in Roman letters. You should have a dictionary and a language guide handy. The *lingua franca* in the tourism sector is English.

Media

In all areas catering for tourism, foreign newspapers are available during the tourist season. In the centres of the major towns, they are on sale all year around at kiosks and international bookshops. Greek radio broadcasts news programmes in English, French and German; television programmes can be received via satellite from other countries.

Postal and OTE Services

In Greece the postal and telephone (OTE) services are handled by separate institutions. Post boxes are yellow and so are the signs outside post offices (*tachythromeía*). During high season, additional mobile post offices are deployed (both post offices and OTE offices are marked on city maps). The hours of business vary from town to town, definite hours being from 8am–2.30pm; in larger towns also until late in the evening (except on Saturday and Sunday). It is possible to make phone calls from most kiosks; telegrams are sent at the OTE offices.

Useful Telephone Numbers

Tourist Information

Chaniá	(0821) 26426
Réthymnon	(0831) 29148
Irákleion	(081) 228203
Aghios Nikólaos	(0841) 22357

Port Authority

Chaniá	(0821) 89240
Réthymnon	(0831) 22276
Iráklion	(081) 226073
Aghios Nikólaos	(0841) 22312

Olympic Airways

Chaniá	(0821) 27701/3
Réthymnon	(0831) 22257
Irákleion	(081) 226073
Aghios Nikólaos	(0841) 22312

ELPA (Automobile Club)

Chaniá	(0821) 26059
Réthymnon	(0831) 29950
Irákleion	(081) 289440
Aghios Nikólaos	(0841) 22620

Greek Mountaineering Association

Chaniá	(0821) 24647
Réthymnon	(0831) 23666
Irákleion	(081) 227609
Aghios Nikólaos	(0841) 24197

Distances from Chaniá to:

Kastélli/Kissamos	42km/26 miles
Réthymnon	72km/45 miles
Hóra Sfakión	72km/45 miles
Omalós	42km/26 miles
Paleóhora	75 km/47 miles

Réthymnon to:

Irákleion	78km/48 miles
Aghía Galíni	62km/39 miles
Amári	39km/24 miles
Moní Préveli	37km/23 miles

Irákleion to:

Aghios Nikólaos	69km/43 miles
Aghios Viánnos	65km/40 miles
Arhánes	13km/8 miles
Festós	62km/39 miles
Kastélli/Pediáda	36km/22 miles
Knossós	5km/3 miles

Aghios Nikólaos to

Sitía	73km/45 miles
Eloúnda	12km/7 miles
Ierápetra	36km/22 miles
Kritsá	11km/7 miles
Moní Toploú	91km/57 miles
Palékastro	94km/58 miles
Zákros	110km/68 miles

Hunting

Hunting is very important to Cretan men. One reason may be because the Turks, during their rule, reserved the right to hunt for themselves – making hunting the free man's prerogative, so to speak. All the same, the dramatic reduction of indigenous species, particularly the nearly complete extinction of the wild goat, the *krí-krí,* has resulted in growing criticism of hunting.

Nude Bathing and Rough Camping

Although prohibited, nude bathing (*yimnismós*) and rough camping are tolerated at some beaches and coves.

Kiosks

It is impossible to picture Greek life without the *períptero*, or kiosk, which sells all sorts of essential little things like cigarettes, newspapers, chewing gum, toothpaste, shampoo, aspirin and ballpoint pens until late in the evening. This is where you will also usually find a telephone.

Sport

First and foremost are the watersports (swimming, diving, wind surfing, sailing, etc). Other popular sports such as tennis are naturally available on Crete as well. In the spring and fall, hiking and climbing in the mountains are particularly attractive outdoor activities. You will also find riding stables near Chersónissos and Irákleion.

Drinking Water

You can drink tap water everywhere except in Irákleion. In the households, drinking water is separate from water for other purposes. It is served with every meal, every sweet dish, each cup of coffee – and is considered a precious treat.

The Greek Language

Greek is a phonetic language. There are some combinations of vowels and consonants which customarily stand for certain sounds, and some slight pronunciation changes determined by what letter follows but, generally, sounds are pronounced as they are written, with-out additions or omissions. Thus, learning the phonetic values of the Greek alphabet, and then reading, say, street sounds out loud, is a good method of getting the feel of the language. Most Cretans have some knowledge of English, and most Greeks are delighted to find a visitor making stabs at speaking Greek. (Unlike Parisians, the Greeks do not ridicule you for making mistakes: they themselves have a hard time with Greek spelling and the complicated Greek grammar.) Whatever you can accomplish, guide book in hand, will be rewarded.

In addition to pronouncing each letter, you should remember that stress plays an important role in Modern Greek. When you learn a Greek word, learn where the stress falls at the same time. Each Greek word has a single stress (marked in the following vocabulary list with an accent). Greek is an inflected language as well, and noun and adjective endings change according to gender, number and case. Case endings, the rules governing them, and the conjugation of Greek verbs, are beyond the scope of a guide.

The Greek Alphabet

CAP.	L.C.	VALUE	NAME
A	α	a in father	alfa
B	β	v in visa	vita
Γ	γ		ghama
		gh before consonants and a, o and oo; y before e, as in year	
Δ	δ	th in then	thelta
E	ε	e in let	epsilon
Z	ζ	z in zebra	zita
H	η	e in keep	ita
Θ	θ	th in theory	thita
I	ι	e in keep	yota
K	κ	k in king	kapa
Λ	l	l in million	lamda
M	μ	m in mouse	mi
N	ν	n in no	ni
Ξ	ξ	ks in jacks	ksi
O	o	o in oh	omikron
Π	π	p in pebble	pi
P	ρ	r in raisin	ro
Σ	σ	s in sun	sigma
T	τ	t in trireme	taf
E	ε	e in keep	ipsilon
Φ	φ	f in favor	fi
X	χ	h in help	hi
Ψ	ψ	ps in copse	psi
Ω	ω	o in oh	omega

Dipthongs

Type	Value
αι	e in let
αυ	av or af in avert or after
ει	e in keep
ευ	ev or ef
οι	e in keep
ου	oo in poor

Double consonants

μπ	b at beginnings of words; mb in the middle of words
ντ	d at beginnings of words; nd in the middle of words
τζ	dz as in adze
γγ, γκ	gh at the beginnings of words; ng in the middle of words

Vocabulary

Pronounce e as in pet; a as in father; i as in keep; o as in oh.

Numbers

one	é-na (neuter)/ é-nas (masc.)/mí-a(fem.)
two	thí-o
three	trí-a (neuter)/tris (masc. and fem.)
four	té-se-ra
five	pén-de
six	ék-si
seven	ep-tá
eight	ok-tó
nine	e-né-a
ten	thé-ka
eleven	én-the-ka
twelve	thó-the-ka
thirteen	the-ka-trí-a/the-ka-trís
fourteen	the-ka-té-se-ra
etc. until twenty.	
twenty	í-ko-si
twenty-one	í-ko-si é-na (neuter and masc.)/ í-ko-si mí-a (fem.)
thirty	tri-án-da
forty	sa-rán-da
fifty	pe-nín-da
sixty	ek-sín-da
seventy	ev-tho-mín-da
eighty	og-thón-da
ninety	e-ne-nín-da
one hundred	e-ka-tó
one hundred and fifty	e-ka-to-pe-nín-da
two hundred	thi-a-kó-si-a (neuter)
three hundred	tri-a-kó-si-a (neuter)
four hundred	te-tra-kó-si-a (neuter)
one thousand	hí-lia (neuter)

Days of the Week

Monday	Thef-té-ra
Tuesday	Trí-ti
Wednesday	Te-tár-ti
Thursday	Pém-pti
Friday	Pa-ras-ke-ví
Saturday	Sá-va-to
Sunday	Ki-ri-a-kí

yesterday	kthes
today	sí-me-ra
tomorrow	á-vri-o

Greetings

Hello	yá sas (plural/polite)
	yá sou (sing./familiar)
	ya (abbreviated)
Good day	ká-li mé-ra
Good evening	ka-li spe-ra
Good night	káli ník-ta
How are you?	Ti ká-ne-te?
	(plural/polite)
	Ti ká-nis? (singular/
	familiar)
fine (in response)	
	ka-lá
pleased to meet you	
	há-ri-ka

Getting Around

yes	ne
no	ó-hi
okay	en dák-si
thank you	ef-ha-ris-tó
very much	pá-ra po-lí
excuse me	sig-nó-mi
it doesn't matter	
	then bi-rá-zi
it's nothing	tí-po-ta
certainly/polite yes	
	má-li-sta
Can I..?	Bó-ro na..?
When?	Pó-te?
Where is..?	Pou í-n-e..?
Do you speak English	
	mi-lá-te ta an-gli-ka
What time is it?	
	Ti ó-ra i-ne?
What time will it leave?	
	Ti ó-ra tha fi-gi
I want	thé-lo
here/there	e-thó/e-kí
small/large	mi-kró/me-gá-lo
good/bad	ka-ló/ka-kó
warm/cold	zes-tó/krí-o
bus	le-o-for-í-on
boat	ka-rá-vi, va-pó-ri
bike/moped	po-thí-la-to/
	mo-to-po-thí-la-to

ticket	i-si-tí-ri-o
road/street	thró-mos/o-thós
beach	pa-ra-lí-a
sea	thá-la-sa
church	e-kli-sí-a
ancient ruin	ar-hé-a
centre	kén-tro
square	pla-tí-a

Hotels

hotel	kse-no-tho-hí-o
Do you have a room?	
	É-hie-te é-na tho-má-
	ti-o?
bed	kre-vá-ti
shower with hot water	
	douz me zes-tó ne-ró
key	kli-thí
entrance	í-so-thos
exit	ék-so-thos
toilet	toua-lé-ta
women's	yi-ne-kón
men's	án-dron

Shopping

store	ma-ga-zí
kiosk	pe-ríp-te-ro
open/shut	a-nik-tó/klis-tó
post office	ta-ki-thro-mí-o
stamp	gra-ma-tó-simo
letter	grá-ma
envelope	fá-ke-lo
telephone	ti-lé-fo-no
bank	trá-pe-za
marketplace	a-go-rá
Have you..?	É-hie-te..?
Is there..?	É-hi..?
How much does it cost?	
	Pó-so ká-ni?
It's (too) expensive	
	I-ne (po-lí) a-kri-vó
How much?	Pó-so?
How many?	Pó-sa?

Emergencies

doctor	ya-trós
hospital	no-so-ko-mí-o
pharmacy	far-ma-kí-o
police	as-ti-no-mí-a
station	stath-mós

'Kalí Stratia' – Farewell

On Crete, when guests depart, they receive a present – a head of cheese, a bag of *paximáthia*, a box full of *kalitsoúnia*, a canister of olive oil, a demijohn of wine, or even *tsigouthiá*. Our gift is a photograph and an anecdote:

A woman, alone in the world (Cháros, the ruler of the Underworld, has taken all her family members) visits the *pappás*, the village priest, and asks, 'Father, father…' 'Go ahead, what do you want?' he replies. 'Can you use *tsigouthiá* as Communion wine?' 'How much have you got?' 'A whole bottle.' 'Oh, then I could use it!' '*Kalí stratia*,' is what one wishes someone just before a trip, whether it be short or long: 'good road'. We wish you that, as well, and '*na mas xanártheteh*' – 'visit us again!'

L

M

N, O

P

ART & PHOTO CREDITS

Photography	**María Síri** *and*
10/11	**Marcus Brooke**
13, 14	**Irákleion Museum**
6/7	**Michelle Macrakis**
Handwriting	**V Barl**
Cartography	**Berndtson & Berndtson**

INSIGHT GUIDES

COLORSET NUMBERS

You'll find the colorset number on the spine of each Insight Guide.

INSIGHT *Pocket* GUIDES

• •
United States: **Houghton Mifflin Company, Boston MA 02108**
Tel: (800) 2253362 Fax: (800) 4589501

Canada: **Thomas Allen & Son, 390 Steelcase Road East**
Markham, Ontario L3R 1G2
Tel: (416) 4759126 Fax: (416) 4756747

Great Britain: **GeoCenter UK, Hampshire RG22 4BJ**
Tel: (256) 817987 Fax: (256) 817988

Worldwide: **Höfer Communications Singapore 2262**
Tel: (65) 8612755 Fax: (65) 8616438

" I was first drawn to the Insight Guides by the excellent "Nepal" volume. I can think of no book which so effectively captures the essence of a country. Out of these pages leaped the Nepal I know – the captivating charm of a people and their culture. I've since discovered and enjoyed the entire Insight Guide Series. Each volume deals with a country or city in the same sensitive depth, which is nowhere more evident than in the superb photography. "

Sir Edmund Hillary